# Using Sartre

*Using Sartre* introduces analytically trained students to the continental tradition of philosophy. Gregory McCulloch relates the early philosophy of Sartre to concerns with which such students are already familiar, such as the mind–body problem, the problem of the external world, freedom and determinism, and the problem of other minds.

McCulloch's distinctive strategy of promoting Sartrean views while working with a resolutely analytical methodology allows him to demonstrate that analytical philosophy, especially analytical philosophy of mind, still perpetuates basic mistakes exposed long ago by the existentialists. Existentialist themes are related to more contemporary interests in analytical philosophy of mind, including the computational theory of mind, externalism and the phenomenology of perception. This enlightening exploration of one tradition using another's methods demonstrates that, despite their mutual antagonism, there is at least one way of bringing both traditions closer together.

*Using Sartre* is a clear and entertaining introduction to Sartre for beginners and non-specialists, sparking a new interest in Sartre's work as well as making a significant contribution to the development of analytical philosophy of mind.

**Gregory McCulloch** is Lecturer in Philosophy at the University of Nottingham. He is the author of *The Game of the Name* (1989) and of the forthcoming *The Mind and Its World* in the Routledge *Problems of Philosophy* series.

# Using Sartre

An analytical introduction to early
Sartrean themes

Gregory McCulloch

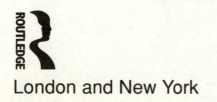

London and New York

First published 1994
by Routledge
11 New Fetter Lane, London EC4P 4EE

Simultaneously published in the USA and Canada
by Routledge
29 West 35th Street, New York, NY 10001

Typeset in Palatino by
Ponting–Green Publishing Services, Chesham, Bucks
Printed and bound in Great Britain by Clays Ltd, St Ives plc
Printed on acid free paper

*British Library Cataloguing in Publication Data*
A catalogue record for this book is available from the
British Library.

*Library of Congress Cataloging-in-Publication Data.*
McCulloch, Gregory
    Using Sartre: an analytical introduction to early
    Sartrean themes/Gregory McCulloch
        p.   cm.
    Includes bibliographical references and index.
    1. Sartre, Jean Paul, 1905–.   2. Existentialism.
    3. Analysis (Philosophy)   I. Title.
    B2430.S34M37      1994
    194–dc20      93–33903
                                                CIP

ISBN 0–415–10953–1 (hbk)

ISBN 0–415–10954–x (pbk)

To the memory of Wal Hansen

'It's no use now shouting across the gulf.'

Michael Dummett, *Origins of Analytical Philosophy*

# Contents

# Preface

This book is an introduction to the early philosophy of Sartre, a 'continental' philosopher, written by an analytical philosopher with analytical readers in mind. Since, despite some positive signs, there is still more truth than there ought to be in the idea that analytical and continental approaches to philosophy are so different that fruitful cross-over is improbable, my intentions need to be made plain.

The Cartesian idea that the mind is a thing in the head (material or not) is alive and kicking in the analytical tradition, and my guiding assumption is that Sartre's anti-Cartesian views deserve more attention than they are wont to receive from philosophers in this tradition. Partly, then, I aim to help counteract what I regard as pernicious philosophical influences by comparing them, unfavourably usually, with doctrines set out with great force by Sartre. People working in the philosophy of mind, I say, would do well to study the early Sartre carefully, and this book is intended to expedite that rather daunting task. The exposition is primarily aimed at undergraduates with a little training in analytical philosophy, and no knowledge of the continental tradition or of French is assumed: but I have hopes that more experienced philosophers, whether or not they are ignorant of this tradition, will find the book worth reading; and if there are any interested non-specialists, then so might they.

It has to be stressed that the methodology I have employed is resolutely analytical. In my view, Sartre repays more aggressive and critical treatment than he receives from the commentators he tends to attract. In a mild sense, then, this is an 'interdisciplinary' book, intended to help in a tiny way to undermine the barriers between analytical and continental approaches by treating Sartre as one of us, and showing that he says things of which analytical philosophers need to take urgent notice. Experience has taught me, however, that I need to repeat that in the analytical tradition, to subject an author's views to prolonged analytical criticism is a sign of respect. Philosophical ideas only really start to live and show their true force when they are put on their mettle. Some people may not be willing to believe this, and so may not consider my intentions towards Sartre to be honourable (someone once remarked that 'McCulloch obviously doesn't like Sartre, because he criticises him'!). Indeed, hardliners on both sides are likely to be uncomfortable about the book's policy of straddling the barriers. Hardliners have a vested interest in keeping the barriers in place: the analytical lot so that they can avoid reading big foreign books, the others so that they can avoid the discipline of organised rational thought. These latter are likely to hate the idea of applying analytical techniques and standards of rigour to Sartre. But the unbiased reader will easily see that I am very sympathetic to much of what Sartre says, as well as to his overall approach. This book is no logic-chopping hatchet-job, intended to justify a smug neglect of Sartre and the continental tradition. The aim is exactly the opposite, to display some of the worth of Sartre and encourage analytical philosophers, beginners or otherwise, to broaden their focus. But, obviously, there is nothing in this either for those who think that analytical philosophy incorporates a bankrupt methodology, or for those who are happy with their focus as it is. Still, analytical philosophers do not *have* to be scientistic bigots, and continental philosophers do not *have* to be sour, uncritical non-theorists. Some people can be expected to read Sartre's texts with goodwill *and* critical attention, and my efforts are directed at them.

Various friends and colleagues have read or listened to versions of some or all of the material, and helped me with their responses. I thank Robert Black, Tim Crane, Jonathan Dancy, Sebastian Gardner, Bob Kirk, Mike Martin, Hugh Mellor, Gabe Segal, Barry Smith, Tom Stoneham, Nigel Warburton (whom I thank for suggesting the final ordering of the material) and the late, sadly missed, Alan White. In the chapters on mental imagery and perception I have benefited from supervising Paul E. Hill's doctoral thesis 'Private worlds and public places' (Nottingham, 1994). I also owe a debt to four generations of Nottingham undergraduates who discovered Sartre with me and helped me to refine my interpretation: I should particularly single out Sarah Firisen, Raj Hazarika and Greg Mason for influencing me on points of substance. I am above all grateful to Rosalind McCulloch for reading an early draft and suggesting numerous improvements.

Chapters 6 and 7 contain material that was originally published in the *International Journal of Philosophical Studies*, vol. 1, and I thank the Editor for permission to include it. I am also grateful to Penguin Books for permission to reproduce the quotation by Simone de Beauvoir on p. 1; to Hamish Hamilton for permission to reproduce the quotations by Sartre on pp. 97 and 120; and to Faber & Faber for permission to reproduce the quotations by Samuel Beckett on p. 52 and by T. S. Eliot on p. 83.

# Abbreviations

TE    *The Transcendence of the Ego*, tr. F. Williams and
      R. Kirkpatrick (New York: The Noonday Press, 1957). First
      published as *La Transcendance de l'ego* in *Recherches
      Philosophiques*, vol. VI, 1936.
STE   *Sketch for a Theory of the Emotions*, tr. P. Mairet (London:
      Methuen, 1962). First published as *Esquisse d'une théorie
      des émotions* (Paris: Hermann, 1939).
PI    *The Psychology of Imagination*, tr. anon. (London: Methuen,
      1972). First published as *L'Imaginaire* (Paris: Gallimard,
      1940).
B&N   *Being and Nothingness*, tr. H. Barnes (London: Methuen,
      1958). First published as *L'Être et le Néant* (Paris:
      Gallimard, 1943).

References to Sartre are to the above English editions (thus:
'TE: 4'). Quotations are taken from the same sources, with the
translation occasionally silently adapted where it seemed important. References to other authors are to be found in the notes about
further reading at the ends of chapters. Uncredited references are
to the present work.

# Chapter 1

# Overview

Aron said, pointing to his glass: 'You see, my dear fellow, if you
are a phenomenologist, you can talk about this cocktail and
make philosophy out of it!'

Simone de Beauvoir[1]

Our exclusive concern is with themes from Sartre's philosophy as
set out between 1937 and 1943, a period when he undoubtedly
produced his most accessible, and arguably his best, philosophical
work. This work is tight and systematic overall, even though its
expression tends to be loose and repetitive. *Being and Nothingness*,
in particular, is a (flawed) masterpiece much on a par with all the
other great philosophical books. It is true that Sartre wrote much
more after the period of concern to us, and there are fascinating
developments and changes to plot.[2] But to introduce the whole lot
digestibly in one breath is probably impossible and would anyway,
I think, obscure rather than emphasise Sartre's philosophical
contribution. The idea is that anyone who works through the
present book will be equipped to do battle with Sartre himself,
early and late. My aim is to extract from Sartre's texts a defensible
and coherent interpretation of his views on consciousness and its
objects, and to present them in such a way that they too, in large
part, may be seen to be defensible, even though they will appear
strange to analytical readers. My guiding thought is that such
readers thus have much to learn from Sartre that is directly
relevant to their own interests.

Naturally, Sartre's work is a response to problems and issues
that he took from the philosophical traditions to which he was
exposed. And to a large extent, these overlap with those encountered by analytical philosophers in the work of the ancients,

Descartes, the British Empiricists, Kant and the logical positivists. So up to a point, Sartre has to be seen as engaged in the same sort of enterprise as any other philosopher. But in making his responses to the traditional issues, Sartre also borrowed from precursors such as Hegel, Husserl and Heidegger, who tend to be little regarded by analytical philosophers, and mixed his borrowings freely into responses of a more recognisably analytical nature. Consequently, much of what he says can appear bizarre or worse to the analytically trained. Moreover, sometimes Sartre's borrowings are mangled, sometimes deliberately warped, sometimes a bit of both. It can be difficult to tell under which heading a borrowing falls, and perhaps even Sartre was not always sure. But his overall presentation and treatment in the early works is more accessible than the work of those he borrowed from, and there is plenty of reason to suppose that working back from Sartre is a less painful, more illuminating introduction to their views and style than is a direct plunge, at least for analytical readers. Thus, as well as helping to correct what seem to me to be inexcusable blind-spots in analytical philosophy of mind, a study of Sartre can also serve as a relatively painless introduction to what seems to have become, shamefully, a different subject altogether.

Sartre's early philosophy has three notable features: a distinctive methodology, a great metaphysical division and some sharply focused aims.

## METHODOLOGY

This owes much to the Phenomenological approach of Husserl and especially to Heidegger's reaction to it, even though Sartre adapted it to his own purposes and was often critical of both authors.[3] The nature of the methodology will emerge as we study the works. But crudely, Sartre is interested in giving a description of, and ruminating in an *a priori*, philosophical manner about, human beings and their world *as they appear to consciousness*, that is *as they are or can be experienced*. Phenomena in this sense – things-as-they-appear-to-consciousness – tend to be seriously misrepresented, if not ignored altogether, by philosophers and scientists whose aim is to account for the reality which is alleged to lie behind and be responsible for the appearances. Sartre correspondingly tends to be hostile both to types of philosophy which ape science, or consider it to be the only source of knowledge, and (especially) to scientific psychology. And we shall see how to vindicate his insistence that reflecting upon the phenomena themselves is intellectually and philosophically respectable.[4] For even if, say, the conscious life of human beings is somehow constituted by their brains and what goes on in them, no description of the neural activity *as such* will tell us what it is like to enjoy a conscious human life.[5] A description of toothache as a certain state of the nerves, for example, will not itself give any clue as to what the toothache feels like, or what it is like to know it as an ache: and this is only the tip of a very large iceberg. Moreover this – its being like something to be conscious – is arguably the most characteristic feature of conscious life, and Phenomenological reflections are thus essential to a complete understanding of it. The issue here, as we shall see at some length, is connected to Sartre's adoption of the idea that understanding persons and their world is a different sort of enterprise from the 'objective' study of nature. Failure to take on board this thought is arguably the principal shortcoming of analytical philosophy.

## A GREAT METAPHYSICAL DIVISION

Sartre usually writes as if there are two fundamentally different kinds of being in the world, namely Being For-itself (*Etre Pour-soi*), or consciousness, and Being In-itself (*Etre En-soi*), or the non-conscious remainder. At first glance, this is highly reminiscent of Descartes' influential dualism of mind and body, according to which there are immaterial minds, whose essence is to think, and material bodies, whose essence is to be extended in space. But it is a very grave mistake to assimilate Sartre's division to Descartes'.[6]

First, one must be aware of what Sartre means by 'being' in phrases like 'Being For-itself'. The word can be used to mean *entity* (as in 'The world is full of human beings'), but Sartre most often uses it in the sense of *way* or *mode* or *manner* of being. Thus, one might describe ordinary day-to-day life as Humdrum Being, or say that beer is an integral part of Tim's very being. So in speaking of consciousness as Being For-itself, Sartre is not thinking of individual conscious agents as entities, but is adverting to the kind of conscious existence which human agents enjoy. He is interested in what is involved, from the phenomenological point of view, in existing (*be-ing*) consciously, rather than in what a conscious entity is (e.g. brain, biological organism, immaterial substance, or whatever).[7] Thus, he later speaks of Being For-others (*Etre Pour-autrui*), and intends here another mode (or 'structure') of conscious existence (see Chapter 8, below). Being For-others is not a distinct entity, additional to the human agent which enjoys Being For-itself, but is, rather, a way of being of such an agent which is made possible by its interactions with others of the same type. According to Sartre, feeling shame is an aspect of Being For-others, since it is only possible for persons to feel this way because others can view them as (shameful) objects in the world: 'Nobody can be vulgar all alone!' (B&N: 222).

A second reason for not assimilating Sartre's distinction to Descartes' dualism is that Sartre, unlike Descartes, denies that his two kinds of Being are really separable. Rather, he holds that they are 'abstractions' from a single reality, 'man-in-the-world' (B&N: 3–4). Third, relatedly, Sartre stresses the extent to which Being For-itself is bound up with the body, and its material history and environment (its *facticity*):

> it is not true that the body is the product of an arbitrary decision on the part of a demiurge nor that the union of soul and body is the contingent bringing together of two substances radically distinct. On the contrary, the very nature of the For-itself demands that it be body.
>
> (B&N: 309)

Fourth, he argues that the mind is not a thing or substance at all (see Chapters 5–7 below). Rather, having a mind is to be understood as a way of being related to the non-mental world or environment. Humans do not 'have' minds in the way that they have kidneys, but they are *minded* in that they enjoy a particular kind of psychological interaction with their situation, an 'engagement with the world' (B&N: 309).[8]

## AIMS

In a nutshell, Sartre seeks to describe and analyse, in a phenomenological vein, the relationships between his different modes of Being. For he holds that they are strongly interdependent: Being For-others requires Being For-itself, Being For-itself is 'founded' on a relationship to Being In-itself, and Being In-itself in turn has at least some of its experienced characteristics in virtue of this relationship. In all this the focus remains primarily on the nature

of consciousness, and what it is to understand conscious phenomena. It will thus be helpful now to move on to some general
remarks about Sartre's view of consciousness. He lays great
emphasis on five distinctive theses about it in almost everything
written in the period concerned. To understand this period of
Sartre's work just is to understand how these theses are supposed
to hang together. These theses are:

1 All conscious acts have intentionality.
2 Consciousness is empty.
3 Consciousness is characterised by, and is the source of,
  nothingness.
4 Consciousness is subject to extreme freedom.
5 There are two fundamentally different modes of self-consciousness or self-awareness.

## SARTRE'S FIVE THESES

1 **Intentionality**   Sartre holds that all consciousness is *of* something – e.g. one sees *a dog*, believes *that it is raining*, imagines *one's
best friend* and so on. The idea is that in all such conscious episodes
there is something – a fact or material thing or whatever – *of* which
one is conscious, and which thus features as the *intentional object*
of the conscious episode. Intentional objects are the things we
think about, see, imagine and so forth. Sartre makes this point by
saying that conscious episodes are 'positional', and that they posit
objects. Thus:

> All consciousness, as Husserl has shown, is consciousness *of*
> something. This means that there is no consciousness which is
> not a *positing* of a transcendent object, or if you prefer, that
> consciousness has no 'content'. . . All consciousness is posi-
> tional in that it transcends itself in order to reach an object, and
> it exhausts itself in this same positing.
>
> (B&N: xxvii)

Versions of this doctrine are widely held by contemporary philosophers, usually in the form of the claim that conscious and other
mental states have semantic or world-involving features.[9] However, there are various complexities involved with the notion of
intentionality about which Sartre says comparatively little. Some
are very important in analytical philosophy, and also bear very

directly on Sartre's own views about Being For-itself and Being In-itself. For example, Macbeth had a hallucination of a dagger, and the natural suggestion is that the intentional object of this conscious episode was a dagger. But there was no dagger present before Macbeth at all, nor need there have been any particular dagger, already known to Macbeth, which he took himself to be seeing. So how can Macbeth's state of mind involve a relation to an intentional object? Such matters will be discussed in Chapters 5–7.

**2 Emptiness**   Although he insists that all conscious episodes posit intentional objects, Sartre also maintains that consciousness itself is empty, that is has no contents, so that nothing is literally *in* consciousness. He does not just mean by this that phrases like 'having x in mind' are idiomatic, with the 'in' not to be taken literally (contrast 'having x in one's pocket'). Given that 'having x in mind' is another way of saying 'thinking of x', or 'having x as intentional object', the denial that 'in' here is to be taken literally would be a way of saying that the intentional object of a conscious event is not actually inside the consciousness in question. Thus

> A table is not *in* consciousness . . . A table is in space, beside the window etc.
>
> (B&N: xxvii)

But he means more than this. According to Sartre, there is *nothing whatever* in consciousness, not even resemblances or representations of its intentional objects. This is most striking in his treatment of visualising or mentally imaging:

> We [have supposed] that the image was *in* consciousness . . . We pictured consciousness as a place peopled with small likenesses and these likenesses were the images . . . This [I] shall call *the illusion of immanence* . . . [the view that] when I 'have an image' of Peter . . . I . . . have a . . . picture of Peter in my consciousness . . . [which picture] is the object of my actual consciousness . . . while Peter, the man of flesh and bone, is reached but very indirectly, in an 'extrinsic' manner . . .
>
> (PI: 2–3)

But his views on perception and other states of mind are in the same vein, as we shall see. Equally, he is adamant that there is no self or ego to be found in consciousness: 'the ego is neither formally nor materially *in* consciousness: it is outside, *in the world'* (TE: 31).

Sartre's Emptiness thesis will occupy us at some length. First, in excluding the self from consciousness, he also, in a sense, denied its existence altogether: the self is a kind of construct only (recall his view that the mind is not a thing), and this is implicated in his radical views on freedom and morality, and also in his view of what it is to understand oneself as a conscious being (Chapter 8).[10] Second, according to one very influential tradition, the mind exists by having *ideas*, which are mental items in the mind, and which are to be distinguished from the things that they are ideas of. When I think about the Eiffel Tower, according to this view, I do so by having an idea (perhaps a mental image) of the tower in my mind, which idea is quite distinct from the huge structure near the Seine. More recently, as the idea that the mind is a kind of computer has taken hold, it has become fashionable to urge that such episodes of thinking are essentially a matter of computational or similar processes involving *representations* of things like the Eiffel Tower in the brain. In many respects, computational representations are just the ideas of the traditional view transplanted into the contemporary context.[11] Sartre's Emptiness thesis is thus opposed both to the traditional view and to current received wisdom in cognitive science and its attendant philosophy of psychology (Sartre says that 'representations. . . are idols invented by the psychologists' (B&N: 125)). Talk of 'the signified', to the extent that this is meant to be something in the mind or brain, is equally at odds with Sartre's thesis.

**3 Nothingness**    In addition to his concern with being, Sartre is also much concerned with non-being or nothingness. He tends to speak of it as though it were a queer sort of real thing, though (we must always remember) by 'real' Sartre usually means *phenomenologically real*, where something is phenomenologically real if it figures in experience, that is if it characterises the way things seem to be. A conscious act or event is separated from its intentional objects by nothingness:

> The structure at the basis of intentionality and of selfness is the negation, which is the *internal* relation of the For-itself to the thing. The For-itself constitutes itself outside in terms of the

thing as the negation of that thing; thus its first relation with Being-In-itself is negation.

(B&N: 123)

Consciousness gets going with a dissociation from Being In-itself. This then involves other kinds of nothingness: for example, absences and unrealised but attainable possibilities, which colour the world as we experience it. My going on holiday to Spain next week is a nothingness, since it is only a mere possibility, which will not be realised. In a sense, so is my jumping to the moon this evening. But whereas the holiday possibility is quite easily attainable, and will remain unrealised only because of my decision to stay in England, the jump to the moon is no possibility for me at all, no matter what I decide. Hence because of the kind of being I enjoy and the capacities I have, the former nothingness, but not the latter, enjoys a kind of experiential reality:

> The world (is) mine because it is haunted by possibilities, and the consciousness of each of these is a possible self-consciousness which I *am*; it is these possibles as such which give the world its unity and its meaning as the world.

(B&N: 104)

As we shall see throughout what follows, such claims constitute Sartre's view that our experience of the world is all of a piece with our activities involving it. This – his *activity-based model of conscious mental life* – is the most notable way in which Sartrean (and other 'existentialist') philosophy departs from more traditional approaches. Sartre's talk of nothingnesses, and also of the attractions and repulsions which we experience things as having, is part of his attempt to convey this novel (and compelling) conception of what experience is actually like.

**4 Freedom**   Where all this activity is concerned, Sartre considers us to be far freer than we customarily suppose: we choose ourselves; we choose what sort of world we shall inhabit; we choose our values. If I choose now not to stay out late tomorrow then I shall have to choose this *again* tomorrow because I always remain free not to do what I have decided. Sartre equates freedom with the ability to 'nihilate' (produce nothingness):

Freedom is the human being putting his past out of play by

secreting his own nothingness; . . . consciousness continually experiences itself as the nihilation of its past being.

(B&N: 28)

The idea, discussed in Chapters 3 and 4, is that Being In-itself plods on being what it is – a stone remains a boring stone until destruction – whereas Being For-itself isn't just what it is (now), since a conscious agent is constantly free to reassess and remake itself, to change its assessment of what it has been (so far).[12] And this capacity for self-assessment in turn contributes to what the agent becomes: there is a feedback effect. If you decide that all along you have been a misunderstood victim, then even if this is a misinterpretation, still the thought may turn you into precisely that kind of person. But according to Sartre nothing in one's past, and nothing in the world of Being In-itself, can force the issue of this or any other sort of personal development. In becoming one is separated from the world, and from one's past (including all past decisions), by nothingness.

Sartre sometimes claims that his views on freedom are opposed to what he calls 'universal determinism', the view that all of our actions and choices are caused, ultimately by events over which we have no control (cf. B&N: 23). Consequently, it is orthodox to bracket him as a libertarian in the traditional debate about freedom, where libertarianism is the view that because we are free, we must be outside the natural order.[13] But whether Sartre really needs to hold a view like this is in fact rather doubtful, as we shall see.

**5 Two modes of self-consciousness**   As already mentioned, Sartre considers all conscious episodes to posit an intentional object. Now among such intentional objects are acts of consciousness themselves. I might think about the Eiffel Tower, and then think about this act itself: 'That's the first time for a week that I've recalled that day in Paris when. . .'. The first act of consciousness, Act 1, which has the tower as intentional object, has here become the intentional object of a further (self-reflective) act of consciousness, Act 2. This mode of self-awareness he calls 'reflective consciousness', or 'thetic self awareness' (B&N: xxix; TE: *passim*; STE: 56). However, Sartre makes a great deal of the point that this is not the only form of self-awareness we enjoy. He claims that in addition to this reflective and explicit self-consciousness, which is just a special case of an act of consciousness positing an intentional object, we are also always at least implicitly self-conscious, in a special way, even when we are not explicitly reflecting. Even while I was engaged in Act 1 above, even before explicitly becoming self-conscious in Act 2, Sartre would insist that I was implicitly aware of myself as thinking about the Eiffel Tower (Act 2 is also thus implicitly self-aware, although it would take an Act 3 for it to become the intentional object of an act: see TE: 44–5). He calls this special kind of implicit self-awareness 'pre-reflective consciousness [or *cogito*]', and also 'non-thetic self-awareness'. Even if my attention is completely absorbed in the intentional object of my consciousness, say this screen now before me, this fact is itself available to me in the non-thetic mode:

> there must be an immediate, non-cognitive relation of the self to itself.
>
> (B&N: xxix)

Sartre links this with what he calls Descartes' *cogito* (e.g. B&N: xxix; STE: 52–4). But he does not mean Descartes' famous argument *'cogito ergo sum'* ('I think therefore I am').[14] Rather, his point is that pre-reflective awareness makes Descartes' argument possible (ibid.). Here he is adopting (and adapting) the Cartesian idea that each of us has, at least potentially or upon careful reflection, a special first-hand kind of knowledge of our own consciousness:

> he who becomes aware of 'having an image' . . . cannot deceive himself.
>
> (PI: 1)

Traditionally, this kind of first-hand knowledge is treated as especially certain, and sometimes also as forming the foundation of all further knowledge. It is doubtful that Sartre intends this elaboration of the doctrine, although it is closely related to the method of the Phenomenologists which so influenced him. In some form or another, it certainly informs his project of analysing phenomena, or things-as-they-appear. This project is discussed below in Chapter 2.

One reason for making Sartre's distinction between types of self-awareness is that assigning intentional objects to states of consciousness is a key part of the phenomenological description of them: concentration on how we posit objects is concentration on what it is like for us to think about and experience things. It is clearly phenomenologically false to suggest that we spend our time thinking explicitly about ourselves and our states of mind: most of the time, our thinking is turned towards the surrounding world. But at the same time, Sartre argued, as mentioned above, that any act of consciousness must always be, in what therefore has to be a special, non-thetic or non-intentional or non-positional sense, aware of its own conscious activity. His argument for this is discussed in Chapter 7.

## NOTES AND FURTHER READING

1  S. de Beauvoir, *The Prime of Life* tr. P. Green (London: Penguin, 1965): 135.
2  See, for example, the helpful collection of essays *The Cambridge Companion to Sartre* ed. C. Howells (Cambridge: Cambridge University Press, 1992).
3  For Husserl's views as they bear most directly on Sartre's concerns, see *Cartesian Meditations* tr. D. Cairns (Dordrecht: Kluwer, 1950); a helpful commentary is David Bell, *Husserl* (London: Routledge, 1990). Heidegger's major work is *Being and Time* tr. J. Macquarrie and E. Robinson (Oxford: Blackwell, 1962); see also the major commentary by Hubert L. Dreyfus, *Being-in-the-world: A Commentary on Heidegger's Being and Time, Division I* (Cambridge, Mass.: MIT Press, 1991). Two helpful and recent general books are David Cooper, *Existentialism: A Reconstruction* (Oxford: Blackwell, 1990), and M. Hammond, J. Howarth and R. Keat, *Understanding Phenomenology* (Oxford: Blackwell, 1992).
4  For a clear account of this style of philosophising, see R. Scruton, *Sexual Desire* (London: Weidenfeld & Nicolson, 1986) ch. 1.
5  For the 'what it is like' of consciousness see Thomas Nagel, 'What is it like to be a bat?', *Philosophical Review* lxxxiii (1974), reprinted in his *Mortal Questions* (Cambridge: Cambridge University Press, 1979) of which chs. 1, 2, 4, 13 and 14 are also illuminating.
6  For Descartes, see his *Meditations on First Philosophy* in, for example, *The Philosophical Works of Descartes*, vol. 2, tr. J. Cottingham, R. Stoothoff and D. Murdoch (Cambridge: Cambridge University Press, 1985). The phrases 'Being For-itself' and 'Being In-itself' are originally Hegel's.
7  Note again that Sartre's interest is in *what it is like to be* conscious, and hence in describing things (both conscious acts themselves, and the things of which they are conscious) as they appear, maybe after a bit of philosophical scrutiny. He is not interested in the 'scientific' question concerning what such things issue from or are made of. To characterise Being For-itself, then, is to describe what it is like to exist as a conscious agent. This is why Sartre subtitles B&N 'An Essay on Phenomenological Ontology'. To the ears of analytical philosophers this sounds paradoxical, because we have come to think of ontology as comprising the job of saying what there is (what entities there are);

and it is natural to think that investigations into what there is must be sharply distinguished from investigations into phenomenology, or how things seem to be (if only because appearances can be misleading). But once it is recognised that Sartre's usage of 'Being' alludes to a concern with ways or modes of being, and once it is accepted that certain things (minds, perceptible objects) can 'be phenomenologically', i.e. exist as appearances, or enjoy a phenomenological mode of existence, the suggestion of contradiction or paradox in Sartre's subtitle vanishes: cf. Dreyfus, *Being-in-the-world* ch. 1.

8   Hazel Barnes gives an accessible account of this in 'Sartre's Ontology', in Howells, *Cambridge Companion to Sartre*: 13–38
9   For a very thorough discussion of intentionality see D.W. Smith and R. MacIntyre, *Husserl and Intentionality* (Dordrecht: Reidel, 1982); and for the contemporary idea that the mind has a semantic or world-involving nature see Colin McGinn, *Mental Content* (Oxford: Blackwell, 1989), ch. 1.
10   An accessible account of some of the issues raised here is given by Christina Howells in Howells, *Cambridge Companion to Sartre*: 318–52.
11   For the traditional doctrine of ideas see Descartes, *Meditations* and John Locke, *An Essay Concerning Human Understanding* Bk II., ed. P. H. Nidditch (Oxford: Clarendon Press, 1975). A useful discussion of the contemporary notion of representation is Robert Cummins, *Meaning and Mental Representation* (Cambridge, Mass.: MIT Press, 1989).
12   Characteristically delighting in a paradoxical mode of description, Sartre often makes this point by saying such things as 'human reality . . . must be what it is not and not be what it is' (B&N: 67).
13   For a discussion of the traditional issues on freedom see Ted Honderich, *A Theory of Determinism* (Oxford: Oxford University Press, 1988) pt 3.
14   Descartes' *cogito* argument appears in *Meditation 2*.

# Chapter 2

# Emotions

Every psychological phenomenon is characterised by . . . intentional inherent existence of . . . an object (by which we do not mean a reality) . . . In the idea something is conceived, in the judgement something is recognised or discovered, in loving loved, in hating hated, in desiring desired, and so on.

Brentano[1]

Sartre took the doctrine of intentionality from Husserl, who got it from Brentano, who picked up the jargon, at least, from the scholastics.[2] Intentional objects, as already remarked, are the things we think about, perceive, imagine and so forth. One way of understanding and developing the doctrine is discussed in the appendix to this chapter, but the most illuminating place to start an investigation into Sartre's approach to intentionality is with his account of emotion. This will enable us to focus immediately on his distinctive conception of experience and the phenomenological (STE is also the most accessible text for the uninitiated).

## EXPERIENCE

Writers in the Cartesian and analytical traditions tend to think of experiencing as a passive affair, in which the world imprints ideas on the contemplating mind. Sartre occasionally talks this way too (e.g. PI: 15), but his considered view is that experience is richer than this, and in particular has an *active* dimension, in that it is a way of interacting with the world and not a way in which we merely contemplate it:

activity, as spontaneous, unreflecting consciousness, constitutes a certain existential stratum in the world.

(STE: 61)

> Perception is naturally surpassed towards action; better yet, it
> can be revealed only in and through projects of action.
>
> (B&N: 322)

This is intended as a general point about being conscious of
intentional objects. Not only is such consciousness, typically,
wholly absorbed in its worldly objects (i.e. it is 'unreflecting
consciousness', rather than reflective self-consciousness), but it is
all of a piece with acting on the things in our surroundings
(unreflecting consciousness is a form of activity):

> When I run after a streetcar ... there is consciousness *of-the-*
> *streetcar-having-to-be-overtaken*, etc. ... I am then plunged into
> the world of objects; it is they which constitute the unity of my
> consciousness; it is they which present themselves with values,
> with attractive and repellent qualities.
>
> (TE: 49)

Three points need elaboration. First, it is 'the world of objects', the
things with which I interact, which helps to constitute the
phenomenology of my experience. Blackbirds and streetcars, and
not little mental pictures of them, feature directly in my conscious
mental life: experience 'goes right up to' its intentional objects. So
to say what it is like for me to enjoy these experiences, you have to
say (at least) what things I am confronting. To understand me is to
see me 'in a situation' (B&N: 293ff.). But, second, because I am an
agent, with preferences and plans, I experience the things I
confront as having certain potentialities ('nothingnesses'). I experience doors and bottles as openable, bicycles as ridable and so
on. Again, then, for an account of my experiences to convey what
they are like, it must get across this aspect of them (cf. B&N:
195ff.). Third, my activities lead me to value and have other
attitudes towards the things I confront. I see things as dangerous
or enticing, to-be-avoided or to-be-embraced. Once again, these
aspects of my experience strike me, according to Sartre, as part of
the scene confronted:

> The immediate is the world with its urgency; and in the world
> where I engage myself, my acts cause values to spring up like
> partridges ... Values are sown in my path as thousands of little
> real demands, like the signs which order us to keep off the grass.
>
> (B&N: 38)[3]

This is Sartre's activity-based model of conscious mental life. How does it bear on the topic of emotions?

## EMOTIONS AND INTENTIONALITY

Characteristically, Sartre stresses the intentionality of emotions:

> The emotional consciousness is primarily consciousness *of* the world . . . fear does not begin as consciousness *of* being afraid, any more than the perception of this book is consciousness of perceiving it . . . the man who is afraid is afraid *of* something.
>
> (STE: 56–7)

In this, he is opposing the idea that an emotion is simply a kind of feeling in the breast:

> it is not a pure, ineffable quality like . . . the pure feeling of pain.
>
> (STE: 91)

He often claims that crucial mistakes stem from failing to note this sort of point (see e.g. TE: 44ff., 54ff.; PI: 76–7; STE: 56–61; B&N: xxviii–xxix). For example, there is a tendency to think of my hatred of Paul as the object of my state of hating him, as if to hate is to be aware of a feeling of hatred (just as to hurt is to be aware of a feeling of pain). But on the contrary, Sartre claims, to hate Paul is fundamentally a way of taking *Paul* as an intentional object. Paul is the object of my state of hating, not some alleged feeling of hatred. I am, he allows, *non-thetically* conscious of hating Paul if I do: but this is not the same as being explicitly, that is thetically, aware of my own feeling (PI: 77; cf. especially STE Part III). And of course I *can* reflect on my hatred of Paul: but that is a further matter. Like believing, imaging and any other mental state, 'emotion is a specific manner of apprehending the world' (STE: 57).

The main point here is absolutely right – 'feelings' of emotion are quite unlike feelings such as toothache or the sting of sunburn – but we do need to quibble. First, must I even be non-thetically aware of emotion whenever I undergo it? Surely people can be angry or jealous, yet sincerely deny it, even after reflection? Yet according to Sartre, to be non-thetically aware of something involves being able to become thetically aware of it after sufficient reflection (see Chapter 7). Second, there can evidently be 'object-less' emotions. I may fear an ogre even though there is no individual which is such that I fear it (see the Appendix for this sort of case). Or I may hallucinate by seeing a tiger and fear 'it': this leads to the Argument from Illusion, introduced in Chapter 5 below. Or I may be depressed or anxious 'about nothing in particular', or afraid but not of any particular thing. Sartre notes such cases, and responds that even then

> it is still *of* certain aspects of the night, or of the world, that one is afraid.

> (STE: 57)

But this is too quick for comfort. Even if some aspect of my circumstances causes me to be afraid, it does not follow that I am afraid of this aspect. Perhaps, in many such cases, reflection would unearth a candidate object, as when someone finally comes to see that fear in the dark is due to having once been attacked at night. But here it seems more accurate to say that this past event is not the intentional object but rather the *underlying cause* of the fear, and it is anyway not guaranteed that a suitable candidate for intentional object will turn up in every case. Think of drugs designed to bring on a general state of depression or euphoria. It is clear that the cause of the state – the drug dose – is not its intentional object, if only because it might have its effect unbeknownst to the subject: and it is not obvious that something else must figure as object instead.[4]

Perhaps Sartre could fairly reply that these are atypical examples. Even when an emotion *does* have an object, however, there are complexities with which he does not concern himself overmuch. An object can be more or less *appropriate* as an object of emotion. An untamed tiger is an appropriate object of fear, an ordinary daffodil is not. Someone who has deliberately and seriously insulted me is an appropriate object of anger, a none-too-bright student is not. Appropriateness of this sort is linked to justification: crudely, appropriate objects of fear are so because they are dangerous or threatening (cf. B&N: 30–1); appropriate objects of anger need to be sufficiently unjust or malicious or negligent. But one must distinguish between kinds of justification. If I have good reason to believe you dangerous, then my fear of you is justified in the circumstances, even if it should turn out that you are not really dangerous at all, so that my fear is not justifiable absolutely. The converse is also possible: you may be dangerous, so that fear of you would be justifiable absolutely, even though no one has any reason to believe that you are dangerous, so that no one could, in the circumstances, justify being afraid of you. These points actually help to vindicate Sartre's claim that emotion is analogous to belief, another 'manner of apprehending the world'. The parallel of appropriateness for belief is truth – only truths are appropriate for belief – and there is again a link with justification, since a false belief might be circumstantially justified (i.e. all the available evidence might support it), and a true (absolutely justifiable) belief might be unjustifiable in the circumstances (i.e. the evidence misleadingly points the other way). Rational belief and rational emotion, then, both come down to what is justifiable in the circumstances: does the evidence available indicate that this matter is an appropriate object of belief/fear? Irrationality in both cases goes with circumstantial unjustifiability. It is as irrational to fear something which you believe to be harmless, as it is to believe something which appears to you to be false on the given evidence.[5]

In another way, though, it can be maintained that emotion itself, even in cases where it is 'justified', is essentially irrational or non-rational. Believing something to be dangerous is one thing, fearing it is something extra, as likely to cloud prudent judgement as it is to facilitate escape. As we shall see shortly, Sartre is inclined to view emotions as non-rational, since (roughly) he sees them as attempts to make insurmountable difficulties disappear by magic. Overall, the issues hereabouts are delicate. Perhaps some emotional responses (e.g. fear, love) are more rationally respectable or defensible than others (e.g. anger, jealousy, hate), even when all are 'justified' (i.e. directed at an appropriate object). Certainly some emotional responses are usually counterproductive, even when 'justified' (e.g. depression). But perhaps we cannot help having emotions anyway, and perhaps it is an Enlightenment illusion to suppose that there could be, even in principle, a supremely rational, non-emotional stance on the world. Still, apart from the question of difficulty-avoidance, none of this is considered much by Sartre, and we shall pass on.[6]

## A 'SPECIFIC MANNER OF APPREHENDING THE WORLD'

Sartre's view is that to be in an emotional state is to stand to an intentional object in a certain way. What way?

His answer draws on his rich conception of the phenomenological. Emotional consciousness 'colours' its objects:

All emotions have this in common, that they evoke the appearance of a world, cruel, terrible, bleak, joyful etc.... [When] I suddenly conceive an object to be horrible ... the horrible is now in the thing, at the heart of it, is its emotive texture, is constitutive of it. Thus, during emotion, an overwhelming and definitive quality of the thing makes its appearance ... The 'horrible' means indeed that horribleness is a substantial quality, that there is horribleness in the world.

(STE: 81–2)

Furthermore, not only is my anger at the bottle which will not open essentially a mental relationship between the bottle and me, but also it involves my physical interactions with the thing. Because I am a conscious *agent*, my experience of the bottle is likely to involve actions on it rather than mere contemplation of it. And these actions, and hence my experience of the bottle, are conditioned by my plans, purposes, needs and wants. I'm thirsty. It's my bottle. My hands are free. So I see the bottle in terms of its possibilities for me: I can grab it, open it, drain it, now. In my circumstances, these unrealised possibilities are real or *live* (see Chapter 3). Although, while they remain unrealised, they are nothing, nevertheless this is the kind of nothingness that is phenomenologically real: it is 'in the heart of being – like a worm' (B&N: 21). These are things I know I can bring about, right here and now, to serve my purposes.

More soberly, one is generally directly conscious of surrounding objects as possible means, ends, things one reacts with (one has a 'hodological chart' of them – STE: 62). But given all this, the world can also be encountered as

difficult, [where this is] a quality of the world given to perception (just as are the paths to the possible goals, the possibilities themselves and the exigencies of objects).

(STE: 62–3)

The bottle will not open, despite my best efforts. Given my aims, I thus experience it as frustrating, unco-operative, malign. Emotion bubbles up: I blow my top and throw the bottle at the wall. According to Sartre, such an outburst

is a transformation of the world. When the paths before us become too difficult, or when we cannot see our way, we can no longer put up with such an exacting and difficult world. All ways are barred and nevertheless we must act. So then we try to change the world; that is, to live it as though the relations between things and their potentialities were not governed by deterministic processes but by magic . . . we fling ourselves into this new attitude with all the force at our command. . . . It is above all the seizure of new relationships and new demands.

(STE: 63)

The crucial point is that because the world is literally mixed in with our consciousness – this is what it means to have a rich, activity-based model of experience – we can get into a frame of mind where we change our way of being conscious as a way of trying to change the world itself:

[emotional behaviour's] aim is not really to act upon the object as it is, by the interpolation of particular means. Emotional behaviour seeks by itself, and without modifying the structure of the object, to confer another quality upon it, a lesser existence or a lesser presence (or greater . . . etc.). In a word, during emotion, it is the body which, directed by the consciousness, changes its relationship with the world so that the world should change its qualities.

(STE: 65)

Emotional outbursts thus have an aim, or *finality* (STE: 48; not to be confused with their intentional objects). You can't open the bottle, so you act out a world where it will open in response to your insults or as a result of being thrown against the wall (anger). You can't get about any more because you are bankrupt, so you act out an undifferentiated world where nothing needs to be done anyway (depression, sadness). You can't elude the tiger so you faint or cower in the corner with your face to the wall, or run away, acting out a world where it is no longer there or cannot simply follow you (fear). One sees the world as 'debased' but also, now, more congenial: anger at the bottle just is a way of seeing and treating it as no longer difficult and unco-operative (although Sartre notes that emotions also normally involve typical physio-logical disturbances such as trembling, flushing, etc. (STE: 76–7)).[7]

Many of these phenomenological claims are compelling, and the theory is intriguing. But some of Sartre's illustrations are far-fetched: the joyful lover anticipating the beloved's arrival dances or sings because he or she is trying, 'by incantation, to realise the possession of the desired object as an instantaneous totality' (STE: 72). Moreover, as Sartre points out:

> This theory of emotion does not explain the immediate reactions of horror and wonder that sometimes possess us when certain objects suddenly appear to us. For example, a grimacing face suddenly appears pressed against the outside of the window; I am frozen with terror.
>
> (STE: 84)

This hardly fits Sartre's theory as so far given because there is no appropriate transforming behaviour to constitute the object as magically debased, nor any build-up of frustration, nor any finality. Nevertheless, Sartre is confident that the theory can cope. What follows is puzzling, although it invokes a thesis about the role of magic in our understanding of human relationships and consciousness to which he often returns. Sartre's view about the face at the window is that just as we can, as it were, put magic in the world by our emotional behaviour, so we can also find it there already, say as the result of the activity of another consciousness:

> the category of 'magic' governs the interpsychic relations between men in society and, more precisely, our perception of others . . . man is always a sorcerer to man and the social world is primarily magical.
>
> (STE: 84–5)

Instead of the agent putting magic into his or her world, the world reveals itself suddenly as a magical environment (STE: 86). This strange-looking but recurrent reference to magic in human affairs, which is linked to Sartre's doctrine of freedom, will be discussed in Chapter 8. It is intimately connected to Sartre's distinctive conception of what it is to understand someone *as a conscious subject*.

Meanwhile, we should ask: on what basis does Sartre put forward this intriguing theory of the emotions?

## THE BACKGROUND: PHENOMENOLOGY AND 'ANTHROPOLOGY'

Regardless of the truth of the account, it is of more than passing interest why Sartre thought of emotion as he did. He intended to see whether one could give an account based on the Phenomenological approach. This involved, among other things, providing a conception of emotion which treated it as meaningful or goal-directed activity, that is activity with finality. On this approach, mental phenomena are seen as making sense in a wider context, as part of an intelligible pattern:

> To the Phenomenologist ... every human fact is of its essence significant. If you deprive it of its significance you rob it of its nature as a human fact.
>
> (STE: 27)

> there is not a taste, a mannerism, or a human act which is not *revealing*.
>
> (B&N: 568)

Not only this, but in giving such an account we can

> take advantage of that absolute proximity of consciousness to itself, which psychologists do not choose to profit by ... and attain and elucidate the transcendent essences of emotion as an organized type of consciousness.
>
> (STE: 22–3)

We can do this because each of us is

> first of all, a being who more or less obscurely understands his reality as a man, which means that I make myself a man by understanding myself as such. I can therefore interrogate myself, and ... carry out an analysis of the human-reality which will serve as a basis for an anthropology.
>
> (STE: 24)

As noted (Chapter 1), Sartre believes our conscious life to be available to us in a special, first-hand way, so that careful reflection on it will give us insight into its nature. Such insights will lead to an 'anthropology', a sense-making account of human beings in the broadest possible terms. Although it would derive from our first-hand way of knowing ourselves, it would not be a recapitulation of received 'wisdom' or common sense, since this sort of pre-philosophical introspective view of ourselves, says Sartre, is 'dim and inauthentic', and in need of being corrected and made explicit by Phenomenological analysis (STE: 24; cf. B&N: 570–1). The result would be to see all human conscious activity, and not just thinking and reasoning, as falling into intelligible and meaningful patterns. We aim for a deeper understanding of what it is like to be us by looking for the finality of conscious episodes.[8] And whether or not every particular facet of human being admits of such an extended understanding, at the bottom of this approach is the idea that understanding someone as a subject of experiences, rather than as a mere object of study for the natural sciences, is a distinct enterprise with its own methodology and criteria for success.[9]

This methodology comes into better focus when deployed by Sartre against 'scientific' accounts of emotion. For example, he dismisses the (Jamesian) idea that emotions are simply consciousness of physiological disturbance on the grounds that this does not reflect the experienced similarities and differences among them:

> the physiological modifications which correspond to anger differ only by their intensity from those that accompany joy . . . For all that, anger is not a greater intensity of joy, . . . *at least as it presents itself to consciousness*.
>
> (STE: 32, emphasis added)

Against a behaviouristic approach (attributed to Janet) which sees emotion as a sort of 'less well adapted' or 'defeated' behaviour he offers a straight dilemma. A young girl sobs uncontrollably on being questioned about some sensitive business. Instead of answering, she exhibits the 'behaviour of defeat'. But the crucial question to ask, says Sartre, is does the girl cry

> *because* she can say nothing . . . or rather, is she . . . crying precisely in order *not* to say anything?
>
> (STE: 40)

And whereas to reply affirmatively to the first half of the question is to offer an account which is 'purely mechanistic', an affirmative answer to the second half

> introduces something new . . .: it alone treats emotion as a way of behaving [i.e. with purpose, not just reactively].
>
> (STE: 41)

We either see the outburst as a mere behavioural effect of the inability to speak, or we see it as part of a pattern of intended speech avoidance (for Sartre's insightful criticisms of behaviourism, see Chapter 8 below). Nor will it do, he adds, simply to posit a neural mechanism linking the behaviours, since this is still 'purely physiological' and hence not at the right sense-making level (STE: 39). Merely to posit a mechanism is not to address the matter of what it is like to undergo emotion, any more than thinking in terms of states of the nerves addresses the matter of what it is like to feel pain.

Sartre seems to be quite right that these approaches are unsuitable if the aim is the Phenomenological one of displaying the finality of emotion. But is it appropriate to take this approach in the first place, and even if it is, is Sartre's the only way to proceed? This raises the thought that sense could be made of the emotional reaction in psychoanalytical terms. Could we not see the girl's reaction as, say, symbolic of an urge to speak of the sensitive matter, which is repressed out of shame? On such a view

> anger or fear are means employed by unconscious urges to achieve symbolic satisfaction, to break out of a state of unbearable tension.
>
> (STE: 49)

Sartre reacts to this suggestion with a critique of the foundations of psychoanalysis. Suppose we say that my emotion is symbolic of a repressed urge. Then this urge cannot be accessible to consciousness: otherwise we have dissimulation or self-deception rather than repression. But then even if the emotion is a sign of the urge, it is 'entirely cut off' from it, as an ordinary effect or natural 'sign' (e.g. a burnt patch of ashes) is cut off from its cause (a fire). And there is 'flagrant contradiction' in regarding a conscious event (emotion) as thus cut off from what it signifies 'unless we regard [it] as an existent of the same type as a stone, or a pond' (STE: 51–2). And this is incompatible with the 'transparent' nature of consciousness:

> in so far as consciousness *makes itself* it is never anything other than what it appears to be. If, then, it has a signification, it must contain this within itself as a structure of consciousness . . . we should look into it for the signification.
>
> (STE: 52–3)

One tool which Sartre is using here is the thesis that consciousness has a special first-hand way of knowing itself. But he actually needs the stronger claim that all *psychological* phenomena (including the significance which this emotion is said to have) must be knowable in this way. And this begs the question at issue, namely whether emotion could have a repressed or unconscious significance. Not only that, but we have already noted that even emotions themselves need not be 'transparent' to the consciousness of those who undergo them (think again of anger or jealousy): so why should their alleged significance be?

Perhaps Sartre has a better argument in reserve, linked to the further idea that there is something special about understanding mental phenomena as such. Think first that if something has significance, then it must be significant *for* someone or something. Spoken sounds and written marks are not significant in themselves – they are just bits of the physical world – but gain significance when beings *take them* so. Then the same should go for an emotion if it signifies a repressed urge: the emotion is constituted as a symbol by being *made to serve thus*. And this presupposes

> an immanent bond of understanding between the symbolization and the symbol
>
> (STE: 53)

– something must take or understand the emotion as signifying the urge. But this must be a single understanding mind. Failing this, we simply retreat to the idea that the emotion is a mere effect of the repressed urge, and lose the right to talk of significance or of symbol. Think here of the difference between boils and rage, both brought about by unacknowledged sexual frustration. The boils are simply physiological effects of the frustration, and even if they indicate its presence, just as ashes indicate the former presence of fire, they are not serving as symbols of the frustration. Similarly, we can either treat the rage too as a mere physiological effect – in which case we are no longer entitled to talk of it as a symbol – or we see it, as even the psychoanalyst sees it, as imbued with meaning or significance. But where there is significance and symbol you need a symboliser, something to understand the symbol. The question then arises who it is that confers the significance on the emotion. We cannot say that an outsider, say the therapist, confers the significance. For although therapists do 'interpret' the subject's state of mind, this is uncovering a significance which the emotion already had. Otherwise, therapy produces the phenomenon it is helping the subject to understand. Alternatively, we might posit several agents in the subject, such as the id, the ego and so on, going in for charades and hiding things from each other. But the problem then is that we lose the human agent who is actually the subject of the emotion that we wish to place in an intelligible context. Each of us becomes, rather, several interacting agents (cf. B&N: 50–4, and Chapter 4 below). In short, given Sartre's belief in a unified subject, *the subject* must be the source of the significance.

This is quite persuasive. Either talk of 'symbols' is out of place, or the account has to become less mechanistic. Either way, the psychoanalytical approach appears unstable. But is Sartre still begging questions by assuming that the symbolising and under-standing have to be *conscious*? Here we should note that practising analysts work to bring repressed urges to the surface, to get the subject to see that rage is a way of expressing unacknowledged frustration, and hence, in a sense, something of his or her own doing (B&N: 574). Such exercises in self-understanding, however fanciful, are not best thought of as involving a mere physiological technique, analogous to the lancing of boils. They are routed through the subject's developing self-conception. Indeed, we are here quite close to the Phenomenological approach to mentality, since for Sartre too the true psychic significance of emotion has to be excogitated, and is neither available to consciousness without effort, nor something to be accounted for in pure physiological terms (see B&N: 458–9). More, he comes to call such sense-making enterprises 'existential psychoanalysis' (B&N: 568ff.). So, in the end, it seems that Sartre's complaints about the psychoanalytical approach to emotion come down to justifiable criticism of the unstable mixture of talk of symbols, on the one hand, and quaint mechanistic metaphors and proliferation of psychic protagonists (id, ego, etc.) on the other.

As for Sartre's own theory of the emotions, the proof of this pudding, as he disarmingly says, is in the eating:

> We have ... to see ... whether emotion ... is in truth a phenomenon that signifies. To come clear about this, there is only one way; that which, moreover, the phenomenologist himself recommends: to 'go to the things themselves'.
>
> (STE: 30–1)

So think about it. Do you debase the world through regarding it as governed by magic when you lose your cool?

## APPENDIX: INTENTIONAL OBJECTS

Sartre's view of intentionality seems in various ways to be different from those of his predecessors, although he says little about the details. But the subject of intentionality is quite puzzling and complex, and the purpose of this Appendix is to indicate a defensible position that would give Sartre all he appears to need. This account concerns the doctrine of intentionality as it has developed in the present century, principally in the analytical tradition. We shall not be directly concerned with expounding Sartre, so the material is optional.

Put simply, the doctrine is that a mental act or state or process, by its very nature, makes a reference to, or is directed at, some further item. A belief, or a piece of knowledge, is belief that such and such, or knowledge that so and so: Galileo believed *that the earth moves*, Einstein knew that $2 + 2 = 4$. In describing these mental items – Galileo's believing, Einstein's knowing – we describe further items. As a first shot, then, we might say that the doctrine of intentionality is the doctrine that mental items are directed at *facts*, such as the fact that the earth moves, or the fact that $2 + 2 = 4$ (cf. TE: 38).

But this is for various reasons an unhappy move. One can believe what is false. Some people believe that the earth is flat, others that it is round. So someone must have got it wrong, and thus, it seems, not everyone has beliefs directed at the facts. People can want what is not the case, and never will be. Hitler wanted to initiate a thousand-year Reich, but it is not a fact that he did so. Wanting the earth to be flat does not make it so.

In reply, one might distinguish between real and unreal facts, and say that false beliefs or frustrated wants make reference merely to putative, unreal facts (note Brentano's claim in the passage at the beginning of this chapter that by 'object' he '[does] not mean a reality'). Then, given this move, it *is* a fact that Hitler initiated a thousand-year Reich, but not a real one. If you like, the fact existed 'in Hitler's world', but not in the real world: it has 'intentional inexistence', to use one of Brentano's scholastic terms, but not real-worldly existence.

As we shall see shortly, talk of unreal entities is too much in need of analysis to be part of an illiminating account of consciousness. But setting this aside, there are anyway problems with the original proposal that mental items make reference to facts, real or unreal. Many mental items seem simply to make a reference to particular things, rather than to facts. I now want *this cup of tea*; my dog fears *the Alsatian down the street*; Queen Elizabeth loves *the Duke of Edinburgh*. Here there seems to be no question of facts being the intentional objects of the states of mind: rather, their objects seem to be individuals like dogs or persons. Noting this, one may now make the following proposal. The intentional objects of mental items really are particular things rather than facts, but some mental items are directed at *more than one such thing in supposed combination*. Thus, whereas the examples just given involve mental acts with single intentional objects, the belief that London is pretty (say) makes reference not merely to the city of London, but also to the property or characteristic of *being pretty*. Similarly, one could suggest that the belief that to be happy is to be well deceived makes reference to the properties *being happy* and *being well deceived*, combined in a certain way. Overall, this proposal avoids talk of unreal facts, and replaces it with talk of real things – individuals (e.g. Queen Elizabeth, London) and properties (e.g. *being happy*) – which may or may not actually be combined in various ways, but which anyway can be thought of as so combined. Or, if you like, a so-called unreal fact is just an envisaged pairing of real things – an individual and a property, say – which does not actually obtain.

However, the spectre of the unreal has not gone away. I may want a sloop, without there being any particular sloop which is the one I want (I have not looked at any sloops, I just want 'relief from slooplessness').[10] So what is the object of this wanting? A sloop? Which sloop? Again, I may want a unicorn for Christmas, or live in fear of an ogre, but there are no unicorns or ogres at all to serve as the objects of these states of mind, nor need I have mistaken any other kind of thing for a unicorn or an ogre. Or I may believe that an engineer assembled my computer, without having in mind any particular person. I arrived at the belief on general grounds.

Once again, one might distinguish between the real and the unreal, this time among particular things rather than facts, and say that the sloop I want, the ogre I fear and the unicorn I want for Christmas, are unreal individuals, which exist 'in my world' but not in the real world. But this will not do. First, the idea of things which do not exist in the real world, but which instead exist 'in the world of' this or that thinker, is very puzzling. What sort of things could they be? How do we manage to direct attention at them? Need they even obey the basic laws of logic? Someone might, after all, want to construct a round square, or go looking for a triangular rectangle. Moreover, I want a real sloop, a real unicorn, not unreal ones. And unreal ogres, ogres that are 'just in my world', cannot hurt me: it is the real ones in the real world that I fear. Of course we do, in some sense, 'think about' such things – this, after all, is one of the facts about consciousness for which we must account. But this is one of the more puzzling facts about consciousness, and if the doctrine of intentionality is to be anything more than a superficial description of an extremely puzzling aspect of the mind, then its proponents had better have more up their sleeve than the present suggestion. In any case, perhaps I believe *truly* that an engineer assembled my computer, so that there is a real individual which is the engineer in question. Even so, thinking about him/her under the vague description 'an engineer' is quite a different conscious phenomenon from thinking about him/her as, say, that person over there, or Dr X.

So here we might try the suggestion that the mental items in these examples have 'indefinite' intentional objects – just *an engineer*, just *a sloop* – and contrast this with cases where the intentional object of a mental state is 'definite' – Queen Elizabeth, Dr X. The trouble now is that talk of indefinite objects is no more perspicuous than talk of unreal ones. On any ordinary under-standing, an indefinite triangle is a vaguely triangular-shaped figure, i.e. not really a triangle at all. But this is not what is meant by the claim that in looking for a triangle I might be looking, not for any particular triangle, but for an indefinite triangle. Fortun-ately, then, it is possible to reapply the above proposal which made theorising in terms of unreal facts unnecessary. We can say that the mental items in question are directed at properties, as before. Instead of saying I want an indefinite sloop or an indefinite unicorn, we can say that I want the properties of *being a sloop* and *being a unicorn* to be instantiated in a certain way (e.g. at the foot of my bed on Christmas morning). We can say that I fear that the property of *being an ogre* is instantiated in a certain way (e.g. at the bottom of my garden), and that I believe the properties of *being an engineer* and *being an assembler of my computer* to be related in a certain way (to be co-instantiated, or had by the same individual). Instead of talking of indefinite objects, whatever they could be, we talk once again of properties and their relations.

So far, then, intentional objects have turned out to be properties such as *being pretty* and individuals such as London, sometimes considered as combined in this or that way. The doctrine of intentionality, on this construal, is the claim that mental acts make reference to such properties and individuals. Unfortunately, the idea that individuals can serve thus leads to some further grave difficulties. For one can reflect on fictional individuals such as Superman. Or, in the factual domain, some confused person might think that there is a certain chat-show celebrity Gore Vidal Sassoon – prophet, ladies' hairdresser, war poet. Others might confusedly wonder whether the present king of France is bald. In these cases we have thought apparently directed at individuals which are unreal or non-existent, and once more we confront the deeply puzzling nature of this state of affairs.

With respect to the last sort of example, which involves a definite description of the form 'the F', it is common to modify the foregoing account of intentional objects, and construe thought about the present king of France (say) as really directed at the property *being a king (of France)*. Generally, one tries to treat thought about *the F* as thought about the property *being F*, which can of course figure as an intentional object even if nothing satisfies it. In effect, this was the import of Russell's influential theory of descriptions, propounded in 1905.[11] Among other things, this saves us again from appealing to the idea of unreal individuals such as 'the' present king of France. And with this advantage in mind, much subsequent philosophical activity has been concerned with examples of the other two types, which involve names (not descriptions) of such 'things' as the fictional Superman and the non-existent polymath Gore Vidal Sassoon. The aim has been to deploy Russell's theory of descriptions so that it can be applied to these cases, and the threatened appeal to unreal individuals avoided here also. For example, Russell and many others have suggested that names are really abbreviations of definite descriptions. 'Superman', on this approach, might be said to abbreviate 'the (fictional) flying avenger also known as "Clark Kent"', and thought 'about Superman' could then be treated as directed at the property *being a (fictional) flying avenger also known as 'Clark Kent'*. This approach brings with it the promise that appeal to individuals as intentional objects can be avoided altogether, and replaced by the sort of appeal to properties characteristic, in effect, of Russell's theory of descriptions. This would enable one to side-step the problems raised by vacuous and fictional names.

However, there is a large tide of literature designed to show that this programme is unworkable because names are not, in fact, abbreviations of definite descriptions.[12] There has developed a corresponding tendency to suppose, at least in non-fictional cases where we are concerned with a *named* (rather than described) existing individual, such as London or Mikhail Gorbachev, that the individual itself can be the intentional object of states of mind. In other words, both properties and (non-fictional, real) named individuals tend to be accepted as capable of serving as intentional objects.[13]

The issues of named non-existents like Gore Vidal Sassoon and fictions like Superman are left up in the air by this move. Furthermore, the whole development of the doctrine of intentionality has been made more complex by the persistent idea that one ought anyway to distinguish between the object(s) of a mental state and its *content*, where the content presents the object(s) in a specific way to the owner of the mental state. Thus the beliefs (a) that Cliff Richard is an eligible bachelor, and (b) that Harry Webb is an eligible bachelor, have the same intentional objects (because Cliff Richard is Harry Webb), even though they are surely different beliefs (not knowing that Richard is Webb, one might defensibly hold belief (a) but reject belief (b)). So, the thought continues, the two names 'Cliff Richard' and 'Harry Webb' must have different contents, that is, present the same man (Cliff Richard/Harry Webb) in two different ways, making it possible to have apparently contradictory attitudes towards, for example, his status as an eligible bachelor.[14] Given the currency of this idea, it is not unusual to read that the true 'objects' of beliefs etc. are contents (propositions and their components), rather than the worldly things that these contents present. This then can be applied to examples such as that of Gore Vidal Sassoon: one might say that 'thought about' this non-existent person involves a content or way of presenting a person which does not, in fact, present anyone at all.

Notwithstanding these complications, it is not misleading to say that the account of intentional objects sketched above, according to which they are properties and named individuals, perhaps as supposedly combined in certain ways, has been developed into the standard contemporary account of what mental (and linguistic) items are about or directed at. This is the view that contemporary philosophers who have considered the matter in any detail are likely to understand as the doctrine of intentionality: indeed, it is one of the glories of analytical philosophy. It is different in various ways from Brentano's doctrine,[15] and not a view explicitly held by Sartre, although I do not think that he could consistently have disagreed with its main drift: on the contrary, I do not see how else his fundamental appeal to the doctrine of intentionality could be secured.

## NOTES AND FURTHER READING

1  F. Brentano *Psychology from an Empirical Standpoint* ed. L. McAlister, tr. A. Rancurello, D.B. Terrell and L. McAlister (New York: Humanities Press, 1973): 88.

2  For a lucid account of Brentano's doctrine of intentionality see David Bell, *Husserl* (London: Routledge, 1990): 9–12, 20–3. For a very thorough treatment of the whole topic, see D.W. Smith and R. MacIntyre, *Husserl and Intentionality* (Dordrecht: Reidel, 1982).

3  Sartre's view here is subtle, as we shall see in more detail in chs. 3 and 4. For even though, as this quote indicates, he believes that we experience value as part of the objective order, he believes that values are also, in a certain sense, *subjective*: 'human reality is that by which value arrives in the world' (B&N: 93).

4  One might here distinguish emotions proper, which by definition have objects, from *moods*, which do not. But this seems to be a trivial linguistic point (why believe that 'fear' denotes two things rather than one?), and it would anyway not help Sartre since his claim is that *all* mental states have intentional objects.

5  It should also be noted that appropriateness for both beliefs and emotion comes in degrees, and that this too is linked to the idea of rationality: it is irrational to be *absolutely terrified* of an ant which might bite and cause minor irritation, or to be *absolutely certain* of something for which there is a little evidence.

6  For a wide-ranging recent discussion of emotion, see R. de Sousa, *The Rationality of Emotion* (Cambridge, Mass.: MIT Press, 1990).

7  See de Sousa, *Rationality of Emotion* ch. 3.

8  It is worth repeating the important point that the finality of a state of mind is not to be confused with its intentional object. Suppose I am depressed because of the state of the nation. Then the state of the nation is the intentional object. But the finality of my state of depression is its alleged ultimate significance, such as an unwillingness to go about my business in an uncongenial world.

9  For a very clear account of this see R. Goldthorpe, 'Understanding the committed writer' in *The Cambridge Companion to Sartre* ed. C. Howells (Cambridge: Cambridge University Press, 1992): 140–77.

10  This phrase is from W.V. Quine's 'Quantifiers and propositional attitudes' in his *The Ways of Paradox* (Cambridge, Mass.: Harvard University Press, 1976). This paper, and the two papers 'On what there is' and 'Reference and modality', reprinted in his *From a Logical Point of View* (New York: Harper & Row, 1961), provide an excellent introduction to a central aspect of the intentionality issue as seen by analytical philosophers.

11 Russell's theory of descriptions appeared in his 'On denoting', *Mind* 14 (1905), reprinted in *Logic and Knowledge* ed. R. Marsh (London: Allen & Unwin, 1956). For commentary see G. McCulloch, *The Game of the Name* (Oxford: Oxford University Press, 1989) chs. 2 and 3.

12 See S. Kripke, *Naming and Necessity* (Oxford: Blackwell, 1980), and McCulloch, *Game of the Name* chs. 4, 8.

13 For these purposes, demonstrative expressions like 'this dog', 'that cat', etc., as used to pick out perceptually available individuals, are regarded as names.

14 Thus, anything figuring as an intentional object does so under a certain guise, or is presented in a certain manner: see G. Frege, 'On sense and reference' reprinted in *Translations from the Philosophical Writings of Gottlob Frege* tr. P. Geach and M. Black (Oxford: Blackwell, 1960); cf. McCulloch, *Game of the Name* ch. 5; N. Salmon and S. Soames (eds) *Propositions and Attitudes* (Oxford: Oxford University Press, 1988), and D.W. Smith and R. MacIntyre, *Husserl* ch. 1.

15 See Smith and MacIntyre, *Husserl*: 40–61.

# Chapter 3

# Nothingness, freedom, anguish

what mainly inspired us with horror and astonishment, was that she bore up under a press of sail in the very teeth of that supernatural sea, and of that ungovernable hurricane. When we first discovered her, her bows were alone to be seen, as she rose slowly from the dim and horrible gulf beyond her.

Edgar Allan Poe[1]

According to Sartre, reflection on the relations between Being Foritself and Being In-itself encounters nothingness at every turn. To confront X as intentional object is to be conscious of *not being* X. Given our plans and aims, the world appears full of nothingnesses such as unrealised but realisable possibilities. According to Sartre's developed account of Being For-itself, consciousness is separated from its past and future by nothingness. More, to be so separated from past and future is to be free, according to Sartre, and freedom is the source of all nothingness. The nothingness of interest is, as it were, a tangible feature of the experienced world. It is not a mere privation, or reflection of the fact that we can make negative judgements. A vivid example is his account of absences. I go to the café expecting to meet my friend but he isn't there. Nor is the Duke of Wellington. As far as their being negative judgements goes, the judgements that my friend is *not* here and that the Duke of Wellington is *not* here are on all fours. But given my expectations, the one nothingness, my friend's absence, has a reality not shared by the other. Whereas the café groups itself around my friend's absence, the Duke does not come into things at all. My friend, but not the Duke, is conspicuous by his absence, which is a real feature of the café (as I experience it). I can *entertain the thought* that the Duke of Wellington is not in the café, but I do not experience his absence: 'It is evident that non-being always appears within the limits of a human expectation' (B&N: 7; cf. 9–11).

What is this all about?

## NOTHINGNESS AND POSSIBILITIES

First, recall that Sartre is usually concerned with phenomenology, so that his point that some nothingnesses are more real than others is not in itself a claim about mind-independent reality: 'more real' often means 'more phenomenologically real' (i.e. more evident to experience). Think of the traditional distinction between primary and secondary qualities.[2] This too is a distinction to do with the perceived qualities of things which turns on whether they involve the existence of minds. Dinner plates standardly appear as both round and white. But, according to the traditional view, whereas the shape of the plates is a primary quality which they have in themselves, the colour is not had by the plates as they are in themselves, but is produced by the light-mediated interactions between their surface properties and our visual apparatus. So colour is not a primary but a secondary quality. Had the visual apparatus or the light been different, the colour too might have been, even though *the plates would not have changed in themselves*. Perhaps our white dinner plates would be blue to Martians in ordinary conditions: perhaps two things which are the same shade of yellow to us would be different colours to Venusians, so that we would be in this respect colour-blind relative to them. Since there is no reason to suppose that one system of colour discriminations is a more accurate reflection of what colour things really are (these Venusians could be red/green colour-blind, despite their prowess with yellow), the correct conclusion is that colour is *relative*.

Up to a point, Sartre is urging that at least some nothingnesses are analogous to secondary qualities in being thus relative. The world appears to us as containing absences and unrealised possibilities, just as it appears to us as containing colours, but in both cases the nature of the appearance is partly a matter of who is being appeared to. 'Objectively' things are not any particular colour, since colour is relative, and 'objectively' my friend's absence from the café is on all fours with the Duke of Wellington's. But add a perceptual system or consciousness with expectations, and the colours and nothingnesses are there to be experienced. Exactly the same goes for values or requirements:

Carthage is *'delenda'* for the Romans but *'servenda'* for the Carthaginians. Without relation to its centres Carthage is no longer anything.

(B&N: 323)

In short, Sartre's claim that some nothingnesses are more real than others should be interpreted as introducing a point about human psychology or (better) what he calls *anthropology* (Chapter 2). If we want to say what it is like for someone to exist as a conscious being, then we must distinguish among unrealised possibilities and absences. Which are the nothingnesses that matter to this person, given his or her plans, projects and expectations?[3]

Sartre is anyway not alone among philosophers in distinguishing different types of unrealised possibility. Imagine here putative states of affairs arranged in a hierarchy. At the bottom are things which just obtain, such as the fact that swans fly. Together with things which do not obtain but which could have, physically speaking, such as a suspension bridge from Dover to Calais, these comprise the *physically possible* states of affairs. At the next step up there are things which could not physically occur but which do not involve self-contradiction (the *logical possibilities*): pigs flying under their own steam, spiders as big as elephants. Finally, there are things which are not even thus logically possible because they are self-contradictory: round squares, standing motionless whilst swimming. These are *impossible* states of affairs. This standard classification is a way of discriminating among nothingnesses, once we ignore the first category of facts which obtain. For the other categories concern facts which do not obtain, that is, nothingnesses.

Another kind of possibility often distinguished involves reference to what beliefs are held by a group or individual. Some things we can envisage, but have no definite views about: as far as we can tell, given what else we already believe, these things are at least not ruled out. For me, it is thus 'open' whether Napoleon had eggs for breakfast on the morning of the battle of Waterloo. Relative to me, therefore, this is an *epistemic possibility*. Now, besides being relative to individuals or groups (perhaps for some people it is not open whether Napoleon had eggs on that morning), epistemic possibilities can arguably come from any of the categories of possibility already mentioned. Clearly, it was at least physically possible for the French commander to bespeak eggs that morning, so this (for me) epistemic possibility is also a physical possibility. But some people think that travelling backwards in time is not ruled out, as far as they can tell. And this is compatible with the idea that time travel is not in fact physically possible. Indeed, it is compatible with the idea that time travel is implicitly contradictory, so that it is not even logically possible.

Sartre's distinction is best seen as a distinction among an agent's epistemic possibilities. Let us fix on *live possibility* as the term (cf. B&N: 41). To make the notion more precise, narrow down my epistemic possibilities – the things that are not ruled out by whatever else I believe, as far as I can tell – to the ones I believe I can now bring about by my own efforts. That excludes building a suspension bridge from Dover to Calais, but leaves in my shaving off my beard. Now narrow down again to the ones which I believe to be means to my present ends. This excludes shaving off the beard, but still leaves in my typing the next sentence. And this remaining class, as a pretty close first shot, comprises an important group of the nothingnesses of interest to Sartre: *things I believe I can now bring about to further my present aims* (this of course also includes my appreciation of the means/end possibilities of the situation: recall the 'hodological chart' of Chapter 2). Absences can then be thought of as a related special case of live possibility. It was not only not ruled out that my friend should be in the café, but it was a state of affairs which I confidently expected to be realised: it was an epistemic possibility of mine which seemed to teeter on the brink of actuality. And this is what marks it out from other unrealised possibilities, such as the Duke of Wellington being in the café. So if we now add the teetering epistemic possibilities to the ones just isolated, we end up with, as an even closer shot, the nothingnesses which I am experiencing in the world. With an important qualification to be introduced later in the chapter, these are a crucial kind of nothingness among those of interest to Sartre.

Acknowledging the phenomenological category of live possibility is an important constituent of Sartre's activity-based model of conscious mental life. Moreover, as we shall see in Chapters 6–8, unprejudiced reflection on how we experience the world shows that this Sartrean model is required. Therefore, we should be more than usually sympathetic to Sartre's superficially bizarre remarks on the topic of nothingness. At least he is trying to be serious and accurate about what it is like to be us. Indeed, he builds a theory of action and its interpretation around this category of nothingness.

An action in the first instance is to be understood in terms of the nothingness it seeks to realise, the *motif* or

> reason for the act; that is, the ensemble of rational consider-
> ations which justify it . . . an objective appreciation of the
> situation . . . the state of contemporary things as it is revealed
> to a consciousness.
>
> (B&N: 445–7)

(*motif* is inexcusably rendered as 'cause' in the standard translation – see B&N: 435n: 'reason' or 'guiding consideration' would be
much happier). My action of switching on my word-processor this
morning has to be seen as guided by my conception of the
nothingness which the present section of this book then was. This
is its *motif*. But a *motif* itself needs to be understood in terms of a
grander design or end (*fin*), which in this case is the completion of
the whole book. This much seems commonsensical. But according
to Sartre we can continue to illuminate the agent by in turn seeing
the *fin* as part of some yet grander design (say, the achievement of
fame and fortune), and so on for quite a bit:

> The problem . . . is to disengage the meanings implied by an
> act – by every act – and to proceed from there to richer and
> more profound meanings until we encounter the meaning
> which does not imply any other meaning and which refers only
> to itself.
>
> (B&N: 457)

What we seek is a 'total relation to the world by which the subject
constitutes himself as a self' (B&N: 563). Here we gradually
become engaged in 'anthropology' or 'existential psychoanalysis',
the enterprise of seeing all human phenomena as part of a wider
meaningful scheme (Chapter 2).

One further ingredient is required in the understanding of an
act, according to Sartre. This is the *mobile* (translated 'motive'),
which is

> the ensemble of desires, emotions and passions which urge me
> to accomplish a certain act.
>
> (B&N: 446)

Thus I switch on the machine (act) because I intend to write this
section (*motif*) due to my burning need (*mobile*) to finish this book
(*fin*) in order to achieve fame and fortune (wider significance) so

people will seek me out (ultimate self-constitution). For Sartre, the essential elements in understanding action are a person-in-a-situation confronted by nothingnesses, and means–end relationships among them, to which attitudes, positive or negative, are struck.

## FREEDOM

But where, asks Sartre, do all these nothingnesses come from? His answer is that

> Descartes following the Stoics has given a name to this possibility which human reality has to secrete a nothingness which isolates it – it is *freedom*.
>
> (B&N: 24–5)

Sartre's view of freedom is related to, but refreshingly different from, traditional concerns with the topic. Minimally, we link freedom with choice. In political terms, being free is often equated with being confronted with options and possibilities for decision. Thus, at a rather shallow level of analysis, people in capitalist societies with full supermarkets are said to be more free than the unfortunates in Bucharest who queue for tickets to queue for beer.[4] But there is a prior linkage between freedom and choice which is presupposed by these political claims. Before we ask what extent of choice is available, there is the matter of what it is even to be capable of being confronted by choice. Trees, boulders and (perhaps) dogs are beyond the pale, since whatever they 'do', it happens without their choosing. In contrast, even the subjects of repressive regimes in barren conditions can still make a choice between the raw potato and the squashed tomato. Unlike the trees and boulders, they at least *can* choose what to do when offered a choice. Politically, we must deplore the way in which their options are cut down. But metaphysically, who can deny their capacity to choose when given the chance?

Sartre's most characteristic views on freedom belong neither on the political nor on the metaphysical level. He does not argue that we are metaphysically free, but assumes it (B&N: 33). He does tend to equate freedom with the capacity (or, indeed, necessity) to choose (B&N: 453 ff.: a characteristic phrase is that we are 'condemned to be free', e.g. B&N: 439, 485). Freedom for Sartre is 'the first condition of action' (B&N Part Four, Chapter 1, section I subtitle) or 'the autonomy of choice' (B&N: 483). But he also often construes freedom as the 'free play of the mind' in considering possibilities (thus Descartes' suspension of judgement on whether there really is an 'external' world – B&N: 25–7). Relatedly, he sometimes regards freedom as a matter of striking attitudes or offering interpretations. You may chain me to the bed, but I remain free to think my own thoughts, reject your evaluations of me, dream about or plot my escape and revenge (B&N: 483–4). Most importantly, a lot of what Sartre says can be interpreted, not surprisingly, as to do with the phenomenology of freedom: with what it is like to experience life as one who must choose.

To see what this means, consider first that any doctrine of metaphysical freedom encounters a fundamental problem. Humans make choices whereas trees do not. But is this enough to ground the *morally* crucial distinction between free and unfree beings? Trees are not free to drop their leaves, so the question of moral assessment of them does not arise. But is it any less a result of natural processes (although more plastic and complex) when I wearily choose to reach over and switch on my word-processor? After all, just as a tree's development is determined by its biological inheritance and the environment in which it plays itself out, cannot the same be said of the human animal's? Each of us is born genetically 'programmed' in various respects, whereupon the long period of nurture begins, during which many of our tastes, beliefs and patterns of response are dinned into us. Well before our emergence as fully developed individuals, we are credited with the capacity to choose and with the related moral responsibility for what we do. But how are we any more than complicated products of gene and environment? And if we are no more than this, why should the matter of moral assessment of what happens have any more application here than it does in the case of the tree?

Philosophers polarise here. Some deny that we are wholly natural beings, perhaps on religious or immaterialist grounds. This makes possible the claim that we are free because, unlike trees, we are thus 'special'. Views like this are called *libertarian*: the idea is that we are free because we are outside the natural or causal order. Others deny that we are in this way 'special', and accept that we are within the natural or causal order: views like this are normally called *determinist*.[5] But here there is a further division, because a determinist, although opposed to libertarianism, need not deny that we are free. For a *compatibilist* is someone who holds that even if we are part of the natural order, still this does not preclude our being free, simply because we (unlike trees) can choose one thing over another. According to compatibilists, the fact that a choice is a natural event brought about by natural means does not preclude it from being an expression of freedom. To be free just is to be able to choose, however naturally. Finally, a *hard determinist* is a determinist who denies compatibilism: to be free requires that one's choices be 'more' than naturally produced events. The hard determinist sides with the libertarian against the compatibilist in holding that freedom requires something special, but disagrees with the libertarian in holding that humans are not thus special. For the hard determinist it is an illusion that we are free, and our practice of moral assessment is especially problematic.

At times Sartre talks like a libertarian, proclaiming opposition to 'universal determinism' (B&N: 26). He says

> by identifying consciousness with a causal sequence indefinitely continued, one transmutes it into a plenitude of being and thereby causes it to return into the unlimited totality of being ... in so far as I [experience nothingnesses] the succession of my 'states of consciousness' is a perpetual separation of effect from cause, since every nihilating process must derive its source only from itself.
>
> (B&N: 25–7)

The free agent 'breaks loose from the causal order of the world; he detaches himself from being' (B&N: 23). This looks like forthright libertarianism. But it is unwise to read too much into this. First, even the talk of 'detaching' oneself from the causal order is given, at times, a phenomenological emphasis. A man may unreflectively put up with his lot because he 'apprehends it in its plenitude of being and ... can not even imagine that he can exist in it otherwise' (B&N: 434). He will not move to change his situation until he has

> give[n] himself room ... to withdraw in relation to it and ... posit an ideal state of affairs as a pure *present* nothingness.
>
> (B&N: 435)

Clearly, this 'plenitude' is not the causal order but the unexamined facts of the individual's life, and the 'withdrawal' is an awakening of political consciousness. Not even a hard determinist need deny that the development of political consciousness involves coming to question what had seemed unchangeable (though he or she might say that the whole process is an illusion). This is not libertarianism.

Second, much of what Sartre says concerns the fact that we face the world as people having to choose what to do, regardless of the metaphysics. From the perspective of the individual, choice faces us most of the time, however much we try to evade it (Sartre, as we shall see, has great insight into the evasions we employ here). Whether or not my choosing to make another cup of coffee just now was a naturally produced event, and whether or not its being natural precludes its being really free, still I had to face it and make it once the thought had occurred. When we confront choice, *che sera, sera* can sound a comfort, but it is in fact no help at all. Thus, against determinism, Sartre complains that it

> is not given as a reflective *intuition*. It avails nothing against the *evidence* of freedom; hence it is given as a faith to take refuge in.
> (B&N: 40)

This phenomenological emphasis is responsible for the fact that Sartre tends to confine his opposition to what he calls *psychological* (as opposed to *universal*) determinism, the view that choices stand to my behaviour just as ordinary causes stand to their effects (B&N: 40, 435 ff.). Although even here he sometimes takes the extreme view that choices do not cause behaviour at all (see STE: 54, and Chapter 8 below), much of what he says has a phenomenological slant. Whether or not my decisions cause my behaviour, they do not *strike me* like that. According to Sartre, nothing we decide to do now, with whatever strength of resolve, is thereby determined to happen, and not just in the trivial sense that something may intervene to stop it (this is true of a stone set rolling down a hill), but in the more interesting sense that one keeps the option of changing one's mind, dissociating from or rejecting the decision, and so on. He illustrates this with the example of a gambler who has resolved never to gamble again, and who finds himself in the casino once more (B&N: 32 ff.). Despite the original decision he remains, in his own eyes anyway, free to gamble. The original decision is set at naught and has to be made all over again:

> freedom . . . is characterized by a constantly renewed obligation to remake the Self.
>
> (B&N: 35)

Of course, such persons may have taken steps to hold their resolve: they might have come out without money, engaged others to act as minders, and so on. But minders can be disengaged, cash dispensers can be found or money borrowed: most of us know how to tell stories like this. So at each moment the original decision is up for review, and is apt to be overturned: we are 'threatened by the instant' (B&N: 466), and

> perpetually engaged in our choice and perpetually conscious of the fact that we ourselves can abruptly invert this choice and 'reverse steam'.
>
> (B&N: 465)

So even if, as universal determinists hold, my original decision causes (along with subsequent events, of course) my ensuing behaviour, it *does not function in my consciousness in that way.* Yesterday's decision – that was yesterday. Today I must either renew it or reject it, in full view of the gaming tables. In itself as it now strikes me it has no power over me, whatever its underlying causal role: it 'stands behind me like a boneless phantom' (B&N: 33). Equally, as I contemplate tomorrow and plan my course of action,

> I at the same moment apprehend these motives as not sufficiently effective.
>
> (B&N: 31)

Tomorrow, all this will have to be gone through again . . . These phenomenological claims are clearly quite independent of the metaphysical debates about whether I am *really* free, and whether or not Sartre intended or realised this.

Sartre goes on that one is separated from both past and future by nothingness. My past does not force me on, my future does not draw me forward. I am separated from both in a void of freedom. As far as my future is concerned, that is just a range of possibilities among which I alone can decide: given my ends and *mobiles*, I need to fasten on to the appropriate *motif*. And the past is no more, along with all my past resolutions. This point about resolutions he links also with his view that consciousness is empty:

as soon as we abandon the hypothesis of the contents of consciousness, we must recognise that there is never a motive *in* consciousness; motives are only *for* consciousness. And due to the very fact that the motive can arise only as appearance, it constitutes itself as ineffective.

(B&N: 34)

We are not 'driven from within', and although he claims that values 'pull us along' he is also clear that, since values have their real origin in us, we do not have to be tugged (see below). This is one component of Sartre's view that consciousness does not contain a self or ego, as it were a nugget of intent or personality which could determine how we are to proceed. He is not here denying, of course, that each of us is a human person, and in that sense a real thing. What he is denying is that the human person is anything more than the conduit through which consciousness expresses its radical freedom.

This central aspect of Sartre's theory of freedom means we must modify our account of live possibility. According to this, recall, my principal live possibilities are (what I believe to be) the unrealised states of affairs which I can bring about to serve my present aims. But Sartre holds that we confront far more live possibilities than this allows. The nothingnesses I most straightforwardly confront are indeed dictated by my aims, preferences and values. And if these were fixed, then the nothingnesses too would be relatively 'hard' features of my world. If I had competing aims to be weighed against one another, I might still confront the world as a place where alternatives exist: the bar is to-be-visited, but the word-processor is to-be-switched-on. Nevertheless, these are still alternatives dictated by my given aims. However, Sartre holds that, because we enjoy the extreme phenomenological freedom just introduced, it is open to us to change or revise at any point our aims and values, to 'reverse steam'. And if we were to do this, then the confronted nothingnesses would change too. Given my present aims, facing this screen seems inevitable. But there is nothing inevitable about this, according to Sartre, because there is nothing inevitable about my present aims, even if they have no given competitors: I am free, he says, to change my aims in any way at any time. In this sense, then, going out for the evening is just as live as facing this screen, for there is nothing inevitable about my keeping the aims which hold me here, any more than there was anything inevitable about the gambler keeping to his resolution. This claim will be examined in the final part of Chapter 4.

## AIMS AND VALUES

So far our discussion of nothingness and freedom has focused on rather mundane aims had by agents, and the live possibilities which they experience as a result. But among the factors which influence the choices of most people are moral considerations, and these are normally distinguished in important respects from other influences on actions. We have just noted that aims often have to be given up, for example if they clash with others deemed more important. We also just noted that, according to Sartre anyway, even apparently unopposed aims are always apt for reassessment and replacement, however inevitable they might seem. But there is a tradition of supposing that morally derived aims are different in these two respects. As far as competing aims (other than competing morally derived aims) go, morality is usually thought to be 'trumps'. It may be up to me to decide whether to go to the football match or to the big fight, but if I have promised to visit my sick uncle instead, there is no similar latitude of choice. It is not in order for me simply to forget about the promise because I'd rather see Leicester City trouncing Liverpool again. Similarly, it is up to me (other things being equal) whether I reassess my long-standing commitment to going to football matches anyway. But, so the traditional thought goes, there is not the same scope for reassessing my commitment to keeping promises. They ought to be kept whether I want to carry on doing so or not. (Whether I should continue to *make* promises is, of course, another matter, as is the question whether I at least have some latitude here.) These claims are commonly associated with the thought that the binding power of morality comes from outside the individual: from God, from Reason, from Objective Moral Reality.[6] But Sartre repudiates any idea of such an external source. His view is that even moral values only have power over me if I let them. And he links this to the view that moral values, anyway, are invented by us, are demands which we put into the world, even though they strike us as objectively there:

> to apprehend the summons of the alarm as a summons is to get
> up . . . to the extent that I apprehend the meaning of the ringing,

I am already up at its summons; [but] it is I who confer on the alarm clock its exigency – I and I alone.

(B&N: 37–8)

Consequently, Sartre holds that I am as free with regard to moral or external requirements as with any other resolution or decision. However fixed and inescapable these requirements may appear – 'I must go, I have no choice, I promised I would' – they are as susceptible to review and reassessment as any other influence on action. If I like, I can forget all about keeping promises henceforth – just like that. There is nothing to prevent me.

In sum, there are two distinctive features of Sartre's account of freedom. The first is that much of it proceeds at the phenomenological level, and is thus largely independent of the traditional political and metaphysical debates. The second is that, at least on this phenomenological level, we are subject to a very great deal of freedom indeed. We confront choice at every turn, not simply with respect to the familiar options – is it to be baked beans or tomatoes? – but also with respect to our past 'firm' resolutions, our most deeply cherished and long-standing projects and, most strikingly, our basic moral commitments.

The question to ask now, of course, is does our way of being really strike us this way?

## ANGUISH AND THE FLIGHT FROM ANGUISH

According to Sartre, the standard conscious manifestation we have of our extensive phenomenological freedom is anguish. Anguish is to be distinguished from fear. Both are responses to threats or dangers, but whereas fear concerns the enemy without, anguish concerns an enemy within:

fear is of beings in the world whereas anguish is anguish before myself.

(B&N: 29)

Thus distinguish the fear of falling from the fear of jumping. I fear the cliff's edge because I could fall, a victim of impersonal causes. So my fear inclines me to keep away from it. But I cannot get away from my inextinguishable freedom to throw myself over if I choose. This I carry with me, and it strikes me as anguish. Again, a soldier going into battle fears the enemy but is anguished at the thought that he might let down himself and his comrades by an act of cowardice. Note, as in the case of the gambler, the point that my resolutions are every moment set at naught. Think too of the stone set rolling down a hill. Once started, only external interference can stop it. But conscious entities carry an extra burden. Not only are they vulnerable, like the stone, to external forces which are thus appropriate objects of fear, but they are also vulnerable to the insidious undermining of resolve which freedom constantly invites. Consciousness in one stroke opens up a world of possibilities, yet at every moment poses their annihilation: this, says Sartre, is our anguished lot. I define myself in terms of my plans and projects, but their implementation depends upon my future self over whom I have no control:

> the self which I am depends on the self I am not yet to the exact extent that the self I am not yet does not depend on the self which I am.
>
> (B&N: 32)

Nor can we draw any strength or purpose from morality, for it too has only the power we decide to let it have.

Note that Sartre does not present us as revelling in our extreme phenomenological freedom, as treating it, as it were, as a great liberation from the cares and constraints of everyday life. This is because of the destructive underside just noted. We generally cherish our plans and projects, define ourselves in terms of our values and overall aims in life. But if these influences on our actions and choices are as insubstantial as Sartre claims, then extreme freedom really is a threatening and self-destroying aspect of our being, and his claim that anguish is the proper apprehension of it becomes more plausible than it initially might seem.

All of this is popular existentialism. But the doctrinal situation here for Sartre is hazardous, and it worsens. His account of freedom is phenomenological, yet his claims about the extent of our freedom are apt to be received with incredulity. Except perhaps in adolescence, we do not normally think of ourselves as constantly remaking ourselves. So the danger is that Sartre's account will not be true to the phenomenological facts. And his talk of anguish is an attempt to ward off this problem by indicating what our consciousness of extreme freedom amounts to. He is fond of mentioning reactions – boredom, nausea, anguish, shame – as constituting consciousness of other things (cf. B&N: xxiv).

Nausea in the eponymous novel is consciousness of the grotesque otherness of the material world (including one's own body, B&N: 338–9). Shame, as we shall see in Chapter 8, is a way of understanding another as a subject of consciousness. Anguish is posed as our consciousness of extreme freedom, as further reflection ought to reveal. Sartre may intend this as one of the things that we are murky and confused about in introspection, which Phenomenological philosophising is supposed to bring to the surface (cf. STE: Introduction; Chapter 2 above). So think about why you feel anguish: isn't it because you need to keep remaking yourself, and might well plump for outlandish or perverse options?

Sartre's doctrinal problem now takes its first turn for the worse. For you may well respond to this question with 'Well, actually, I don't feel very anguished at the moment: I hardly ever do'. Yet if Sartre is right about freedom, and about anguish, it might seem that we should be anguished nearly all of the time, since we are nearly always having to decide what to do. But as he himself points out, anguish 'is completely exceptional'. So how, he immediately asks, 'can we explain the rarity of the phenomenon of anguish?' (B&N: 35). By way of preliminary, he notes that much of the time we are absorbed in activity: more, that we often do not realise what our possibilities are until we find ourselves acting them out. Thus, the more we act in a blind or mechanical or habitual manner, the less we have explicit plans about which we can feel anguish. Recall here the distinction between thetic and non-thetic self-awareness (Chapter 1). If I aim to turn on the light, then I am (thetically) aware of the switch as an instrument of my design and (non-thetically) aware that I am – I could acknowledge that this is my aim if prompted, and perhaps after consideration. But I need not be reflecting explicitly on my state of switch-directed awareness, and normally I will not be. Somewhat relatedly, we must distinguish *feeling anguish* from *being subject to anguish*. According to Sartre, we are subject to anguish as we go about our daily affairs, even if we do not always feel it: rather as one might be subject to depression while a small diversion causes momentary cheerfulness. To feel the anguish to which I am subject, I 'must place myself on the plane of reflection' (B&N: 37) because 'anguish . . . is the reflective apprehension of freedom by itself' (B&N: 39).

Sartre further draws on his idea that moral values strike us as objective, rather than as motivations within. This, he goes on, enables us to overlook the fact that we are the real source of these values, and so to treat them as pulling us along inexorably (recall 'Values are sown in my path as thousands of little real demands' (B&N: 38)). At the limit, we become 'serious'. The 'serious' person, of whom Sartre invariably writes with scathing contempt, is one who believes that values are fixed or unrevisable. According to Sartre,

> the serious man . . . apprehends values in terms of the world and . . . resides in the reassuring, materialistic substantiation of values. In the serious mood I define myself in terms of the object by pushing aside *a priori* as impossible all enterprises in which I am not engaged at the moment; the meaning which my freedom has given to the world, I apprehend as coming from the world and constituting my obligations.
>
> (B&N: 39–40; cf. 580)

Given this, the phenomenon of 'ethical anguish' – the realisation that values are not really efficacious except in so far as I will them to be – 'is a secondary and mediated phenomenon' (B&N: 38). It is something which only reflection will turn up, like ordinary anguish.

However, this is very far from the end of the matter: we are now on the brink of an abyss. For Sartre next notes that we are prone, even after awakening from our 'serious' slumbers to face our extreme freedom, *to attempt to evade it*. We pretend that we have an essence or personality that obliges us to behave in certain ways. We pretend that the anguish-inducing possibilities – that I could jump off this cliff, that I needn't do the decent thing – are mere logical possibilities rather than live ones (B&N: 41). We formulate determinism, the view that we have a pre-ordained inner nature which determines what we shall do, as a scientific or philosophical evasion of the issue of anguish and freedom, a 'faith to take refuge in' (B&N: 40). Importantly, Sartre's view is not that we are mistaken about these things, but that we really know the score yet choose to ignore it. The thoroughly modern person, who knows that God is dead, who knows about the Great War, Hitler, Stalin, Hiroshima, Pol Pot . . . – the thoroughly modern person knows that the world is in its essence valueless, and that any meaning it has for us is put there by us.[7] And, the thought continues, what we have put into the world we can take away, replace with something different. So Sartre means to be taken quite literally when he talks of evasion. In one sense, people (educated ones anyway) know the extent of their freedom, and are thus subject to anguish which they would feel if they let their minds dwell on the matter. But the prospect is too painful, so evasive strategies are employed. Now Sartre's problem gets even worse. He says that

It is certain that we can not overcome anguish, for we *are* anguish. As for veiling it, aside from the fact that the very nature of consciousness and its translucency forbid us to take the expression literally, we must note the particular type of behaviour which it indicates. We can hide an external object because it exists independently of us. . . . But if I *am* what I wish to veil, the question takes on quite another aspect. I can in fact wish 'not to see' a certain aspect of my being only if I am acquainted with the aspect that I do not wish to see. . . . In a word, I flee in order not to know, but I can not avoid knowing that I am fleeing; and the flight from anguish is only a mode of becoming conscious of anguish.

(B&N: 43)

If we really do know that we need constantly to remake ourselves, then attempts at evasion are attempts at a form of self-deception, says Sartre.

And unfortunately, self-deception is a puzzling if not paradoxical idea.[8] To deceive you about something, I need to believe it myself yet at the same time induce you not to believe it. So to deceive myself I need to believe something yet at the same time induce myself not to believe it. And this looks like a contradiction. How can I believe and not believe the same thing at the same time? And how could I take myself in? After all, if you know I am trying to deceive you then I will not succeed. Imagine playing yourself at chess, and trying to sneak a checkmate as white. This surely cannot be done unless you stop trying as black. Yet self-deception, on the other hand, is analogous to the situation where you somehow both try to sneak the checkmate as white and *don't notice* as black. All the same, Sartre considers himself to be committed to the view that this sort of apparently contradictory state of affairs is extremely common, since most of us, according to him, know in our hearts the true extent of our freedom yet refuse fully to acknowledge it to ourselves. Most of us live in a state of what he calls *bad faith* about our freedom most of the time: an extremely unwelcome result if, as he generally assumes, bad faith about freedom involves self-deception.

Sartre's complicated response is one of the more celebrated parts of B&N, and to this we shall now turn.

## NOTES AND FURTHER READING

1  Edgar Allan Poe, 'Manuscript found in a bottle', *Selected Writings* ed. D. Galloway (Harmondsworth: Penguin, 1967): 104.

2  See John Locke, *An Essay Concerning Human Understanding* ed. P. H. Nidditch (Oxford: Clarendon Press, 1975) bk. II, ch. VIII, ss. 8–26.

3  There is a somewhat different debate about the being of unrealised possibilities. When I say 'There is a possibility that pigs should fly', ought this 'there is' to be taken literally, as in 'There is a spider in my soup'?

Since this latter sentence can only be true if a certain thing, the-spider-in-my-soup, exists, must we also say that the former sentence is true because a certain (possible) state of affairs, pigs-flying, also exists, even though it has not been realised (i.e. is a nothingness)? This is a philosophical question to do with the kind of being enjoyed by certain nothingnesses: see D. Lewis, *On the Plurality of Worlds* (Oxford: Blackwell, 1986). As it happens, Sartre's concern seems to be neutral with respect to this particular question. *For whether or not* one grants that unrealised possibilities exist, it is still left open that talk of possibility is legitimate. After all, we accept that it is legitimate to talk of doing something 'for Jim's sake', even though we are unwilling to grant that *sakes* are things which exist, alongside tables and chairs and sticks and stones. We are uneasy about thinking of Jim's sake as a thing on a par with Jim's baby: still, talk of Jim's sake is clear and unproblematic. But if it is in a parallel way granted that talk of unrealised possibilities is legitimate even if *they* do not exist, then it is left open that Sartre might successfully distinguish among them in some interesting fashion to do with how we experience the world, and quite independently of the existential question. Recall once more that the 'reality' of nothingnesses in which Sartre is interested is *phenomenological* reality. Yet another related issue concerns the *likelihood* of this or that unrealised possibility. Thus we say that one nothingness (a certain smoker's death from cancer) is more likely than another (her growing a chimney). But is this because she actually has a potential or propensity or objective tendency to contract cancer, given that she smokes, or is it simply a reflection of our expectations, so that saying 'it will probably happen' is just a way of saying 'we confidently expect it to happen'? Here Sartre sides with the latter idea:

> Being in-itself cannot 'be potentiality' or 'have potentialities'. In itself it is what it is – in the absolute plenitude of its identity . . . The possible comes into the world through human reality. These clouds can change to rain only if I surpass them towards the rain.
>
> (B&N: 98)

4  One might also distinguish here between freedom *from* certain kinds

of interference, and freedom *to* do certain things: see I. Berlin, 'Two concepts of liberty' in his *Four Essays on Liberty* (Oxford: Oxford University Press, 1969).

5 This name is not entirely appropriate, since some aspects of the natural order may be indeterminate or random. But a libertarian need not find any comfort in this: if what I do happens at random, then I am no more 'special' than an electron.

6 See D. McNaughton, *Moral Vision* (Oxford: Blackwell, 1988).

7 See R. M. Hare, *Freedom and Reason* (Oxford: Oxford University Press, 1963), pt. I.

8 See P. Gardiner, 'Error, faith and self-deception', *Proceedings of the Aristotelian Society* (1969–70).

# Chapter 4

# Bad faith and self-deception

... whole body like gone ... just the mouth ... like maddened ... so on ... keep ... what? ... the buzzing? ... yes ... all the time the buzzing ... dull roar like falls ... in the skull ... and the beam ... poking around ... painless ... so far ... ha! ... so far ... all that ... keep on ... not knowing what ... what she was ... what? ... who? ... no! ... she! ... SHE!

Samuel Beckett[1]

The position we have reached is this. Sartre has claimed that

1 as conscious agents we have extreme freedom,
  and inferred that

2 we are conscious of this freedom,
  a claim which he construes as

3 we are always subject to anguish.

  But (3) is in some tension with the evident fact that

4 we only exceptionally feel anguish, *even after reflection*,

  and Sartre moves to release this tension with the claim:

5 we are always subject to anguish, but typically pretend not to notice.

It is in order to explain 'pretend not to notice' that Sartre has to tackle the question of self-deception, since pretending not to notice implies that you have noticed.

There are, of course, various other strategies for easing the tension between (3) and (4). One is to deny (1), Sartre's claim about extreme freedom. Here one treats the tension engendered by (1)–(4) as a *reductio ad absurdum* of that claim. Naturally this could not be seen as much of an option by Sartre, but we shall return to it ourselves below. Alternatively, one might refuse the step from (1) to (2): why should we realise that we are extremely free, even if we are? But this would strike even deeper to the heart of Sartre's procedure, since his aim is to give a phenomenological account of the things which concern him, and if we are (phenomenologically speaking) as free as Sartre claims we are, then this ought to be available to us, at least after suitable reflection. A better move would be to deny that (3) is an appropriate construal of (2): why should we be conscious of extreme freedom by being subject to anguish? But it is doubtful whether this could give him everything he needs. Suppose we forget about anguish, and treat consciousness of extreme freedom as simply the capacity to *say* upon reflection that we are extremely free. The fact remains that few people seem to have reached this point. Explicit subscription to Sartre's conception of freedom is, if anything, even rarer than anguish. So there would still be the problem of explaining the apparent evasion. One could reply that the world still awaits the dawning: the full implications of the conclusion that the world in itself has no meaning have not filtered through yet. People just have not realised the consequences this has for our freedom and our values. Now this may have some truth as regards uneducated people, although even here one meets corner-shop relativism as often as Clapham omnibus certitudes. But in any case, there are educated people who ought to be aware of extreme freedom but who busy themselves in what Sartre is obliged to call evasion. Universities, British ones anyway, are hardly angst-ridden existentialist hotbeds. Rather, Sartre would say, they tend to be complacent and disingenuous sources of psychological determinism and similar evasive doctrines.

Is there anything left for Sartre? Short of abandoning his view of freedom, or his phenomenological aspirations, is he condemned to confront the paradox of self-deception? One thought is that bad faith about freedom might be explained in terms of muddle or confusion rather than self-deception. One would treat 'bad faith' as a technical term for our complex attitude, *whatever it is*, to our extreme freedom. This would leave it open whether bad faith, so understood, really does involve self-deception, and so leave room for replacing (5) above with

5\* we are always subject to anguish, but typically fail to realise this due to muddled thinking or confusion.

And there is a hint of this in Sartre's treatment, as we shall soon see. We shall also see that this is all to the good, since although Sartre's analysis of bad faith is of wider import than a mere attempt to overcome a large technical hitch in his apparatus, and is typically penetrating and insightful, nevertheless he certainly does not solve, or even make a credible attempt at solving, the problem of self-deception.

## SELF-DECEPTION

The problem, as Sartre notes, is that self-deception cannot be glossed as lying to oneself:

> The ideal description of the liar would be a cynical conscious-ness, affirming truth within himself, denying it in his words, and denying that negation as such . . . [But] the liar intends to deceive and he does not seek to hide this intention from himself.

Yet, on the other hand,

> There must be an original intention and a project of bad faith; this project implies a comprehension of bad faith as such and a pre-reflective apprehension (of) consciousness as affecting itself with bad faith. It follows . . . that . . . I must know in my capacity as deceiver the truth which is hidden from me in my capacity as the one deceived [and all at the same time too].
>
> (B&N: 48–9)

One knows yet does not know: this is bad enough. But given the translucency of consciousness, the self-deceiver must be (non-thetically) aware of what is going on: and then 'this whole psychic system is annihilated' (B&N: 49). How can there even be room for deception when the dupe actually knows about the attempt at deceit, not only on reflection, but as part of the attempt? How can you trick yourself at chess? It thus appears that

> we can neither reject nor comprehend bad faith
>
> (B&N: 50)

The phenomenon is so hard to understand that it is tempting to cave in, and to try to say that it is not really possible at all. What people go in for, we might say, are exercises in more or less stable incoherence and muddle. They are well aware of the true state of affairs, or are at least capable of becoming so, but they simply avoid thinking about it too much, or at all. They are not so much self-deceived as lazy and forgetful, insincere and muddled, fond of a drink. But it is difficult to square this with a sensitive exposure to the facts. Most of us, either from our own case or from literature, have evidence that real self-deception is possible.[2] Still, this leaves room for a partial cave-in on the part of Sartre. We should remain clear that Sartre's own problem is to square his doctrine of extreme freedom with the phenomenological facts, and resorting to the idea that self-deception is involved here is not obviously obligatory. Perhaps, as already noted, there is room for an account of bad faith with respect to freedom which is cast in terms of muddle and incoherence. Nevertheless, Sartre persists in representing himself as having to deal with the real paradoxical thing.

## THE UNCONSCIOUS

He thus turns to attempts to explain self-deception in terms of the unconscious: for example, the idea that some mechanism is at work which only allows certain facts about the subject to come into consciousness. This, he claims, is in effect to replace

> the duality of the deceiver and the deceived, the essential condition of the lie, [with] . . . that of the 'id' and the 'ego'.
>
> (B&N: 51)

On this view, one (unconscious) part of my mind deceives another. But then, Sartre objects, why should people under analysis resist the process, as they characteristically do? Who is doing the resisting? Not the conscious ego, since it wants to know what is going on, and not the unconscious id, since it has been doing its best to spill the beans by producing the appropriate kind of symbolic behaviour! So perhaps it is the censor, which stands between the ego/analyst and the id. The id tries to make things manifest, the censor sees the damage this would cause to the ego, and so it only allows veiled symbolic expression. The id knows I can do what I like, the ego would be anguished if it found out, so the censor allows the id to cause me to make a great fuss about wearing an unsuitable hat. But on this model, says Sartre, the censor itself is now self-deceiving, since it both knows about what is being withheld from the ego, yet at the same time denies it. This, says Sartre, is just to relocate the problem (B&N: 53).

The criticism is unconvincing. There is nothing odd about the censor resisting analysis, since its aim is to prevent the ego from knowing the truth. This need not involve self-deception. If I know that Bill is cheating Sally, yet prevent him from making it too obvious to her, I am at worst a conniver.

However, one feature of the appeal to the unconscious is that it threatens the unity of the agent as a psychic entity. It would not be *me* who (1) is subject to anguish because of what I realise about freedom, (2) takes steps to conceal this fact and (3) resists attempts to bring the matter to light. In effect, this approach dissolves the problem of self-deception by denying the existence of self-deceiving agents. Each of us would be two, three or more agents in one body. Sartre objects that this 'breaks the psychic unity' (B&N: 54). This is not an inconsistent appeal to the existence of a self, but rather a commitment to hang on to a Phenomenological approach to the mind. As such it may look question begging, but in so far as we have had experience of what self-deception is like, perhaps we can justifiably reject an attempt to dissolve the unity of this experience.

If we dismiss psychoanalytical approaches, Sartre continues, then the only course left is to

> examine more closely the patterns of bad faith and attempt a description of them ... [which] will permit us perhaps to ... reply to the question ... 'What must be the being of man if he is to be capable of bad faith?'
>
> (B&N: 55)

And with this he launches into his celebrated analyses of individual cases.

## TRANSCENDENCE AND FACTICITY: BEING'S TWO FACES

His overall idea is that we are capable of the paradoxical state of self-deception because we are, in a sense, deeply contradictory beings: Being For-itself 'must be what it is not and not be what it is' (B&N: 67), and 'bad faith requires ... that there be an imponderable difference separating being from non-being in the mode of being of human reality' (B&N: 66). More specifically, Sartre's account rests on a playing-off against one another of two doctrines. One is his thesis that we are subject to extreme freedom or transcendence (with its corresponding denial of psychological determinism), and the other is his view that we exercise our freedom subject to *facticity*, or the constraints of our material and bodily circumstances. The doctrine about freedom is opposed to the idea that we have a nature or essence which determines how we should act or live. But the doctrine of facticity concerns how we are constrained by things: the 'coefficient of adversity' of our material surroundings, our own bodily form of existence, our past decisions and choices which have brought us to where we are now. Somehow we surpass or transcend essence-governed Being In-itself, yet at the same time we are hemmed in by it, physically and temporally: 'On all sides I escape being and yet – I am' (B&N: 60). Bad faith comes about because of this

> double property of the human being, who is at once a *facticity* and a *transcendence*. These two aspects of human reality are and ought to be capable of a valid co-ordination. But bad faith does not wish either to co-ordinate them or to surmount them in a synthesis.
>
> (B&N: 56)

To be in the mode or manner In-itself and to be in the mode or manner For-itself are utterly different things. Let us write the first as 'to BE' and the second as 'to **be**'. An inkwell is an inkwell in the manner In-itself: so an inkwell IS an inkwell. A waiter is a waiter in the manner For-itself: so a waiter **is** a waiter. But it is not true that an inkwell **is** an inkwell (or anything else), and it is not true that a waiter IS a waiter (or anything else). Ordinary language is confusing because it only has the one verb – 'to be' – where in reality it needs two if Sartre's fundamental distinction in Being holds: 'to BE' and 'to **be**'. As Sartre puts it, the concept of being is 'two-faced' (B&N: 67). Not only this, but Sartre's principal idea is that this fundamental ambiguity or two-facedness is playing a crucial role in the cases of bad faith he discusses. The state of bad faith

> must affirm facticity as *being* transcendence and transcendence as *being* facticity, in such a way that at the instant when a person apprehends the one, he can find himself abruptly faced with the other.
>
> (B&N: 56)

Thus a waiter, or a grocer, might act out a stylised waiter/grocer routine, making exaggerated gestures and flourishes in the one case, humbly wiping the dust off a tin of beans in the other. Moreover, Sartre goes on, we tend to like and expect this sort of thing because 'a grocer who dreams is offensive to the buyer' (B&N: 59). However, these stylised routines might represent attempts to become absorbed in the role, and so to enjoy a thing-like, choiceless existence: BEING a grocer or waiter. But, Sartre insists, this is impossible: even a waiter is free, so cannot BE a waiter.[3] Although there is a sense in which a waiter *is* a waiter (rather than a diplomat) – he **is**, by choice, a waiter – this must not be confused with the way in which an inkwell IS an inkwell:

> as soon as we posit ourselves as a certain being . . . we surpass this being – and that not towards another being but towards emptiness, towards nothing.
>
> (B&N: 62)

Several things, according to Sartre, make it easy to blur the distinction between BEING and **being**, and hence open the way for bad faith. First, when my existence is considered from the point of view of another person, I am, up to a point, just an object in their world (cf. B&N: 381). Hence a waiter, 'expected' just to BE a waiter-thing, might easily slip into taking the role too seriously. But here he is in bad faith. This and other aspects of our Being For-others will be examined in Chapter 8. Second, however, there is a deeper sense in which I am an object in another's world, since one way to encounter me is as a flesh and blood animal body. This makes it possible for me to try to enact this version of myself. Sartre illustrates this with the example of a woman who tacitly acquiesces in the sexual advances of a man, whilst pretending to herself that in taking hold of her hand he is merely admiring her in a platonic sort of way. According to Sartre she is trying to turn herself into a body-thing in his hands. Unwilling to acknowledge her welcome of his sexual interest, she tries to BE putty in his hands. The self-deception arises because she is really just **being** passively receptive (B&N: 55–7). Third, one anyway cannot take on a job or career without accepting some limitations on how to proceed. A waiter is a waiter rather than a diplomat. So there is

> the obligation of getting up at five o'clock, of sweeping the floor of the shop before the restaurant opens, of starting the coffee pot going etc.
>
> (B&N: 60)

Waiterhood carries with it its own facticity, and so makes room for the attempt to deny that I choose 'to confer their urgency upon my duties and the rights of my position' (ibid.).

Fourth, there is an undeniable fixed aspect to a person's past choices and behaviour which stand behind them in a thing-like way. Hence at one point Sartre says that 'my essence is what I have been' (B&N: 450), and although he acknowledges that past episodes are partly left open to be interpreted in the light of what follows on (B&N: 498ff.), still he is clear that a free being 'can not give itself any past it likes according to its fancy' (B&N: 496). Rather, 'the past is the ever growing totality of the In-itself' 'which has slowly congealed and solidified around us'. At the moment of death, indeed, 'the For-itself is changed forever into an In-itself' (B&N: 115). So we are constantly and increasingly weighted down towards the thing-like in virtue of our past choices, and here, correspondingly, is yet more scope for confusion between BEING and **being**. One may identify too closely with all that has gone before, and 'forget' that the future still has to be chosen, and that one may still reverse steam. Nevertheless, Sartre insists,

> so long as we are not dead, we are not this In-itself in the mode of identity. *We have to be it* . . . [that is, we] reassume it at each moment and sustain it in being.
>
> (B&N: 115)

I **am** my thing-like past but I cannot BE it while alive. I am responsible for it as long as I live: but I can still surpass it.

This fact about our relationship with our past introduces a rather different source of bad faith. So far we have been concerned with the attempt to deny **being** and embrace BEING: but a sort of opposite can occur too. Sartre illustrates this with a man who, from the ample evidence available, 'is just a homosexual' (B&N: 63ff.). He is sexually attracted to men rather than women, and unequivocally expresses this preference in his sexual behaviour. He too is, of course, well aware of these facts. Yet he resists the simple and obvious conclusion, perhaps because he has some implicit sense of guilt. He is always ready with a rationalisation of his sexual conduct: despite the obvious, he is not 'just a homosexual' – things are far more complicated than that! At every turn he resists and obstructs the verdict. This man is in a state of self-deception to the extent that he realises the true import of his behaviour, while also apparently believing the rationalisations he offers.

According to Sartre, this man's self-deception is made possible by his exploiting the difference between the *true*

1  It is not the case that I AM a homosexual

and the *false*

2  It is not the case that I **am** a homosexual.

Statement (1) is true because, as a free being, he cannot BE anything – that is the mode of Being In-itself. So although his past behaviour has laid down a facticity of homosexuality which is visible to anyone who wants to see it, still whilst living he is free to throw off his sexual preferences and reverse steam, says Sartre. At the same time, however, his past choices ensure that (2) is false, because he manifestly **is** a homosexual: in the mode of 'having to be it' or Being For-itself, he has adopted that path so far. So although he can truly say 'I AM not a homosexual', he cannot truly say 'I **am** not a homosexual'. Unfortunately, confusion is possible because ordinary language lacks the two verbs. Our man justifiably says 'I am not a homosexual' on the strength of the truth of (1), but takes or represents himself thereby to have successfully contradicted the claims, based on the falsity of (2), of those who observe his sexual behaviour. Sartre's view is that this man is using his freedom to remake himself as a way of not taking responsibility for what his free choice has brought him to so far: in saying, quasi-justifiably, 'I am not a homosexual' he 'plays on the word being' (B&N: 64). He is dishonestly distancing himself from his past choices, and the facticity they have imported into his life, by concentrating solely on his freedom to reverse steam.

Sartre mentions an important factor at work in such rationalising projects (B&N: 67–70). Few if any beliefs exist without evidence that counts against them. Equally, evidence can be cited for the most outlandish views. These facts always enable one to run an implausible line in a discussion, say, and to escape definitive refutation, as long as one is prepared to be bloody-minded enough. Plenty of people who know that the world is round would be unable to give a satisfactory explanation of why things do not fall off the bottom. No doubt they would vaguely cite their faith in expert opinion, to the delight of the flat-earther, who can then point to the 'obvious' fact that we stand on a flat (though bumpy) plane. Irritated, you simply turn away, and – there you are, the flats have it! This fragility suffered by belief is also exploited by self-deceivers. At the outset of their project they

> [do] not hold the norms and criteria of truth as they are accepted by the critical thought of good faith . . . [They stand] forth in the firm resolution *not to demand too much*.
>
> (B&N: 68)

Once this has started it is self-propelling:

> One puts oneself in bad faith as one goes to sleep and one is in bad faith as one dreams. Once this mode of being has been realised, it is as difficult to get out of it as to wake oneself up.
>
> (ibid.)

Our homosexual can keep going in his self-deception because no claim about his past behaviour is immune from reinterpretation given enough ingenuity: and one rationalisation suggests another. . .

Bad faith, in sum, essentially involves placing too much emphasis on facticity or too much emphasis on transcendence. One might expect, then, that good faith involves facing up to our true situation, and giving each aspect of it its due in a 'valid coordination' (B&N: 56). But even here lies scope for further bad faith. This concerns sincerity or truth-to-oneself, the apparent opposite of self-deception. According to Sartre, it is in fact 'a phenomenon of bad faith' (B&N: 63). Imagine the homosexual's friend, who more than anything wants him to face up to his sexuality and thus to be true to himself by acknowledging that he 'is just a homosexual'. This friend is guilty of an error parallel to that of the self-deceiver, according to Sartre. He wants the homosexual to acknowledge what he is, as a step on the way to redemption ('a sin confessed is half pardoned' (B&N: 64)). Until he faces his homosexuality, he is just a slave to it, and is cut off from his self or true nature. But the friend here overplays his hand, says Sartre. Certainly, the homosexual **is** a homosexual, but acknowledging this is no way of getting nearer to the ultimate truth about himself or his true nature, since there is no such thing: it is not the case that the homosexual IS a homosexual, or indeed anything. As a conscious agent he cannot BE anything. He has no true nature to be true to or to be cut off from. Thus what can be the significance of the ideal of sincerity except as a task impossible to achieve . . . And this impossibility is not hidden from consciousness; on the contrary, it is the very stuff of consciousness . . . How then can we blame another for not being sincere or rejoice in our own sincerity?

(B&N: 62)

Even the attempt to be honest with oneself is a snare for the unwary, another potential refuge from extreme freedom.

## SO WHAT IS THE SOLUTION?

All of this is insightful and fascinating. But we now ought to step back and take stock, and ask what exactly the solution to the problem of self-deception is supposed to be, and whether it succeeds.

It must be said first that there is a danger of a play on words in the remarks on sincerity. If you persistently deny that you are a homosexual by offering rationalisations of your actions, then there is nothing muddled or dishonest or self-deceiving about trying to get you to see this. Sincerity, in this sense, is simply a willingness to speak plainly about the overall tendency of one's ways as evidenced by past behaviour. There need be no tempt-ation to think that this tendency is somehow unwilled or thing-like, an inescapable aspect of one's unchangeable underlying nature. All that is needed is a recognition that one's behaviour has so far fallen into a certain pattern, freely chosen if you like, and that attempts to obscure or break up this pattern with flim-flam and rationalisation are dishonest or at least inaccurate. Indeed, the very possibility of good faith or 'valid co-ordination' presumably requires this sort of sincerity. Some champions of sincerity may overshoot by thinking in terms of fixed person-alities or underlying natures, but that is by no means obligatory. It is one thing to have a method of classifying behaviour in terms of the manifest plans and intentions of the agent concerned ('he's only here for the guys'), and another to suppose that this reflects a fixed nature (cf. Sartre himself at B&N: 65–6).

Be this as it may, Sartre's view is that self-deception involves either our avoiding the fact that our mode of existence is to **be** by trying to believe that our mode of existence is to BE, or our taking refuge in extreme freedom and denying our past deeds.

What is not clear is how to apply this to the case that prompted the discussion, namely our alleged failure to confront the fact that we are subject to anguish. Indeed, the answer appears to be too easy: we avoid the anguish by supposing ourselves to exist in a thing-like way. This is too easy because it does not elucidate our attitude to freedom and anguish, but merely restates it. Nor does the example of the homosexual, with its facticity-denying form of self-deception, appear to be doing any work. Nor has the phenomenon of self-deception been made any easier to understand. All we have been told is that it comes about because we somehow exploit the two-facedness of being.

To see what the problem is here, all we need to do is ask whether this slippage between modes of being is something we deliberately engineer, or something that comes about because of unclarity of thought with regard to **being** and BEING. If the second, then bad faith has been explained without any ultimate invocation of the paradoxical notion of self-deception: people living in bad faith with respect to their freedom are just the victims of a logical or conceptual muddle, like the comical participants in political debates who use 'refute' to mean *reject* but who still suppose that in saying 'I utterly refute that claim' they have not only not accepted it, but also somehow managed to undermine it. And this second approach is better than the alternative, which involves the idea that we deliberately engineer such confusions between BEING and **being** as are relevant to our living in bad faith. For if this is so, then it is easy to see that we have got nowhere. For these deliberately engineered confusions could only serve their purpose – that of shielding us from the anguish of our extreme freedom – if we believed in the confusions thus engendered. Hence in engineering such confusions we should need to deceive ourselves over the import of the effort. And this is itself a self-deceiving project, the very thing Sartre set out to explain.

The second, 'muddle' explanation fits in with some of Sartre's procedure, although it does not, of course, square with his repeated claims that bad faith with respect to freedom involves self-deception. Nor does it square with his suggestion that we 'forge expressly to persuade ourselves' the two-faced concept of being (B&N: 67), nor with his claim that projects of bad faith rest on a 'decision . . . on the nature of faith [i.e. on standards of evidence]' (B&N: 68). But then perhaps Sartre has no firm grip on what he wants to say. It is instructive here to review the example of the homosexual, which has turned out to be so curiously irrelevant. By hypothesis, he is deceiving himself over his sexuality, and his friend can be accused of muddle over the two-facedness of being if we stipulate that he loads the notion of sincerity appropriately. But it is not obvious that the homosexual is similarly muddled, and there is no reason to charge his friend with self-deception. The homosexual may have some ideal of human sexuality which he cannot bear himself not to live up to: hence guilt and self-deception, but no bad faith over freedom. And the champion of sincerity may be muddled over the matter of unchangeable human nature: hence bad faith over freedom, but no self-deception.

It seems that Sartre cannot have it both ways: either bad faith is non-self-deceiving muddle over the two-facedness of being, or it is engineered and hence self-deceiving muddle, and the element of self-deception has been left completely unanalysed.

## WHAT TO DO?

Does the problem of bad faith arise anyway? Certainly there is a problem about self-deception, whether or not Sartre's notion of bad faith involves it: self-deception is a problem for everyone, since it is a paradoxical notion. But is there really a problem about bad faith with respect to freedom? This comes down to the question, is Sartre right about our extreme freedom? For if he is, then there is a problem about our lack of acknowledgement of it, even after reflection, and whether or not the acknowledgement consists in our being subject to anguish. But if we are not as free, phenomenologically speaking, as Sartre says, there is no problem.

To say that we are subject to extreme freedom is to say that we are free to change even our values, and basic aims and projects. One reply is that this does not fit the phenomenology, and not because of any muddle, but because it underplays the fact that values and desires can have increasing degrees of entrenchment in an individual's mode of being. As I now see things, I could certainly throw over my plan to go out tonight, especially if something more important cropped up. But take my long-term aim of continuing as a professional philosopher: I do not feel even slightly free to give that up. I once remade myself in a fairly drastic way by deciding to pursue this goal, so my present state is something I willed and for which I am responsible. Also, I am continually reaffirming the project, at least implicitly, since it guides the choices I make and gets me out of bed in the morning. I would strongly resist, by choice, efforts to separate me from my career. But I do not feel free to throw things over, and I do not seem to be confused by the two-facedness of being. I accept that I cannot BE a professional philosopher, realise I **am** a professional philosopher, but still do not feel that I can change this. I accept that it is *logically* and *physically* possible that tomorrow I should throw it all in, but I cannot see it as a *live* possibility, as a possibility *for me*.

Similarly, I cannot see any way of quelling my moral approval of the rescuers of abandoned donkeys. But this is not to be 'serious'. I fully accept that the world in itself is, in Einstein's phrase, a pile of dirt (or something like that), and that meaning and value only come into things because there are evaluators. But, first, this does not entail that values are either chosen, or up for overthrow. The world in itself is not any particular colour, but colours are not chosen, and are not up for overthrow (short of surgical intervention, perhaps). Thus, one might claim that although values are put into the world by evaluators, they tend to become ingrained and not under the control of the will. Nor need this involve the claim that evaluators have a fixed nature which causes them to BE evaluators of a certain kind. The point is compatible with the idea that different people embrace different values (think of different types of colour vision).

Second, in any case, the claim that values become entrenched is compatible with the thought that we choose them, say as teenagers. The present issue is not about how we get our values and projects, but about how we keep them, and what scope we have for revising them, phenomenologically speaking. To the extent that values and projects are chosen, one may properly be held responsible. I am responsible for my decision to become a professional philosopher: that is the sort of person I am. But it does not follow that I can see as live the option of throwing it all in to do something else instead. Even though I chose this course, and constantly reaffirm it by my local plans and actions, thereby freely continuing my assent, so that there is no compulsion here – even so, it does not follow that I see the abandonment of my career as a live option, even after reflection. One may reply that I am not really free if I cannot see my way clear to change, and that my conduct resembles the progress of a drunk: the result of free choices, but now beyond the scope of the will. However, this point is irrelevant. For it is directed at the metaphysical question of what freedom consists in, rather than at the phenomenological question of what possibilities strike one as live. Sartre, *qua* libertarian, might be tempted by this argument. But it is still irrelevant. Furthermore, it would be dangerous to take this line, since that would be effectively to concede that career change for me is no live possibility: and this involves denying that I am subject to extreme Sartrean freedom (phenomenologically speaking).

Some of Sartre's talk of choice is anyway over-blown. We have just seen that to choose something is not the same as to be able to give it up later, even if it is a source of responsibility. But conversely, not everything that makes a person what they are, and is a source of responsibility, is something they chose. Someone might just have drifted into a career without reflection. They may now every day 'reaffirm' their commitment in much the way that I, who explicitly chose my career, do, and so in this sense are to be held responsible for what they are. But they neither chose what to become nor need they be able to choose to desist. We have acknowledged all along that freedom has some link with choice (or the capacity to choose, anyway), but it is not the link sometimes suggested by Sartre. This point is most glaring in his notorious claim that each of us makes an 'original choice' about the type of person we are to be:

> This original choice operating in the face of the world and being a choice of position in the world ... brings together in a prelogical synthesis the totality of the existent, and as such it is the centre of reference for an infinity of polyvalent meanings.
>
> (B&N: 570)

This invites a charge of incoherence – how could I make an original choice unless I already existed as some sort of person? – and encourages the comment that perhaps we are, after all, partly made by initial conditions outside our control, and so not as free as Sartre supposes. But this is a double confusion. *Of course* we do not make an 'original choice': we initially just grow into things. Yet this has no bearing at all on the question of how free we are, phenomenologically speaking, that is, on whether we can see our way clear to change what we have grown into. At another point Sartre says

> Even this disability from which I suffer I have assumed by the very fact that I live; I surpass it toward my own projects, I make

of it the necessary obstacle for my being and *I cannot be crippled without choosing myself as crippled*.

(B&N: 328: emphasis added)

Similarly, a person under torture 'has determined the moment at which the pain became unbearable . . . Thus he is entirely responsible for it' (B&N: 403). On the face of it this is just silly. If I am born without legs I do not choose this as I might choose, say, to have wheels fitted. And although I might 'make of it an obstacle' by deciding on a career in ballet, I did not make it the obstacle to the very conduct of my life. Why then does Sartre say such apparently silly things? Because he does not really mean them. The passage about disability goes on:

> This means that I choose the way I constitute my disability (as 'unbearable', 'humiliating', 'to be hidden', 'to be revealed to all').
>
> (B&N: 328)

Here the point is clearly to do with attitudes taken in the face of the disability, with how one decides to play the hand dealt. And although even here we might wonder how much scope there is for choice given the gravity of the affliction, it is true that in so far as the subject is evaluated as a person, their attitude to disability contributes to what sort of person they are. If you 'give in' to your misfortune, then we can sympathise, but still that is the sort of person you are.

Think now of all the possible determinants of our aims which are rooted in our biological facticity. Because of an in-built tendency to perform acts conducive to reproduction, I have more than religious objections to becoming a monk: celibacy is no live option for me. Notice how contentious Sartre's example of the homosexual actually is. Do people really choose or have the live possibility of changing their sexuality? Is it not, rather, that some people find themselves sexually attracted to men, others to women and some to both?[4] Certainly, if one is to be straightforward, then sexuality is the sort of thing that has to be taken responsibility for, and this contributes to the sort of person you are. But choice and change are other matters entirely. Again, the fact that we need food and drink to survive helps to give us the tastes and preferences that in turn influence our plans and projects. I see no way of evading my standing desire for curry, which leads me freely to keep well stocked-up with spices. The fact that some people can mortify the flesh is not, of course, any argument that I could, any more than apostates from the cause of donkeys show that my views here are subject to overthrow. Once again, the claim is not that there is a universal and environment-independent thing called 'human nature' which leads each of us to have the same tastes and preferences (or would if it were not distorted by political or other factors). The point is simply that the broad kinds of preference we have are influenced by bio-logical and chemical factors and do not strike us as the 'boneless phantoms' of Sartre's account.

Another possible source of confusion concerns Sartre's ten-dency, briefly noted in the previous chapter, to think of freedom as the 'free play of the mind', citing Descartes' sceptical questioning of his belief in the material world as an example. Perhaps the intended parallel where aims and values are concerned is to do with at least being able to envisage alternatives. Perhaps someone incapable of this is not really a fully paid up moral agent (think again of 'seriousness'). But from the fact that we can adopt a questioning attitude towards our values, nothing much follows about our capacity to see them as really changeable. Even if I am brought to acknowledge that my esteem for donkey lovers is somewhat idiosyncratic, still I may not see any way of giving it up. There is no necessary translation into action. I may subsequently find myself a bit absurd at times, or modify the way I describe things, or just forget about the episode, but there need not be any further change in which possibilities I regard as live. The parallel with Descartes is actually rather damaging to Sartre. We cannot really help believing that we have arms and legs, even after we have read Descartes and seen how difficult it is to resist the sceptical charge that this belief is insupportable. Whether or not we come to think that we have an answer to scepticism, we do not really give up our belief, even if, in certain contexts, we *say* 'I have no way of telling whether I have arms and legs'. Similarly, I might be brought to the point of saying 'this donkey business really is absurd', even as I sign my cheque to the charity. All of this may betray a lack of high seriousness, but the fact remains that the 'free play of the mind' has only a limited success in changing our actions and attitudes to things.

So the phenomenological case for extreme freedom does not seem especially compelling, and as far as we have been able to tell this is not due to muddle over the concept of being. All these possibilities which, according to Sartre, should at least eventually strike me as live, remain stubbornly dead, mere logical or physical possibilities of no concern to me. Still, there are plenty of good things to be said about Sartre's treatment. People do have a despicable tendency to shelter behind things rather than accept responsibility for themselves. 'I did it because I am at bottom a nasty person' is both logically incoherent (being nasty cannot be your *reason* for doing something) and morally evasive (you did it to hurt her). People spinelessly blame their parents or their circumstances, or cite authority or abstract allegiance, and try thus to disown or disguise their own choices and actions (and especially the consequences: 'It's X's fault that I blew up an innocent bystander while opposing him/her/it'). Sartre's scathing dissections of bad faith and 'seriousness' are absolutely to the point here, and in so far as his doctrine of extreme freedom boils down to a plea for straightforwardness and good faith, it is certainly to be embraced.

Moreover, we are also a lot freer than we usually realise, phenomenologically speaking. Cowardice, inertia, sloppy-mindedness, humbug or plain habit are among the things which lead us not to regard as live possibilities which really are live (recall the case of political awakening from Chapter 3). It can come as a massive revelation that long-standing habits or values, increasingly the cause of discord and frustration, can be thrown off just like that. Other apparent immovables need to be worked at over a period, but eventually succumb. But now one can imagine Sartre picking up on this very point. Perhaps even my career as a professional philosopher is not completely immune to overthrow, given a careful and prolonged effort. I could start by thinking about what I could do instead . . .

Perhaps not. Still, if we accept the Sartrean claim that we are at least freer than we usually think, how is one to distinguish live possibilities which do not immediately seem so from possibilities which are not live at all? Because our tastes and values can and do change over time, possibilities which do not now strike me as live may become so as a result of successive changes. Does that show that these possibilities are 'really' live for me now, even though they do not strike me as such? Presumably not: I suppose that it would at least be required that I should be able now to see these remote possibilities as aims which I could gradually and intelligibly work towards having. But as far as I can tell, that still rules out career change, celibacy and many other possibilities which Sartre would insist are live.

## NOTES AND FURTHER READING

1  S. Beckett, *Not I*, in *The Complete Dramatic Works* (London: Faber & Faber, 1973).
2  For a characteristically harrowing study see Patricia Highsmith, *This Sweet Sickness* (Harmondsworth: Penguin, 1972).
3  Sartre's views echo somewhat the traditional distinction between *accident* and *essence*. My car is both green and a motor vehicle, but whereas we can easily envisage changing the car's colour without destroying it, things seem otherwise in the other case. For example, if we melted the car down and fashioned its material into a large typewriter, then the car would be no more. Thus my car *is essentially* a motor vehicle, but only *accidentally* green. Up to a point, Sartre can be seen as saying that a Being For-itself has no essential, but only accidental, features. Thus a waiter, for example, *is accidentally* but not *essentially* a waiter. Elsewhere, he makes his famous claim that 'essence comes after existence' where persons are concerned: people are not brought into existence with a pre-set essence or nature, unlike (say) motor cars, inkwells and paper-knives (B&N: 468). Rather, their 'essence is suspended in [their] freedom' (B&N: 25). The one thing which cannot be chosen is this freedom: although 'we can even choose not to choose ourselves' (B&N: 472), still 'not to choose is, in fact, to choose not to choose' (B&N: 481). However, the analogy with traditional talk of accident and essence should not be pressed too far. First, my car is only accidentally green, as we said, but this does not mean that it is free to remake itself a different shade. Second, I am arguably – and Sartre would not have demurred here – essentially an enmattered being. But even if this is so, there is no real objection to Sartre's claim that I have no essence. For he means that I have no *psychological* essence, at least as things strike me, and this is compatible with the thought that I have some non-psychological essence, such as being enmattered, as a consequence of being human.
4  Sartre's example is (no doubt deliberately) very provocative. Contrast a case such as that of a sexist or racist. One need not have chosen to take on sexist or racist attitudes, since they may have come with one's education, and one's society may be steeped in them. But it is highly appropriate, as well as desirable, to try to get such a person to change them in the light of the obvious rational and moral objections to them. But even if there *were* rational and moral objections to, say, homosexuality, it is much less plausible to suppose that sexual preference falls similarly within the scope of such types of persuasion.

# Chapter 5

# Imaging

> The yarns of seamen have a direct simplicity, the whole meaning of which lies within the shell of a cracked nut. But Marlow was not typical . . . and to him the meaning of an episode was not inside like a kernel but outside, enveloping the tale which brought it out only as a glow brings out a haze, in the likeness of one of those misty haloes that sometimes are made visible by the spectral illumination of moonshine.
>
> Joseph Conrad[1]

We turn now to Sartre's activity-based model of conscious mental life itself, having noted at some length how it ties in with his general methodology and his theory of action. The truth is that as an approach to *experience* it is extremely difficult to get a clear view of. As remarked in Chapter 1, it is the principal way in which 'existentialist' philosophies depart from tradition, and we shall ultimately see that there is much to recommend this radical departure.

## IMAGING AND INTENTIONALITY

Most of us can visualise things, or picture things to ourselves, and Sartre's account of this is no less striking than his theory of emotions. First, he brings the doctrine of intentionality to bear in a forthright fashion:

> whether I see or imagine that chair, the object of my perception and that of my image are identical: it is that chair of straw on which I am seated. Only consciousness is *related* in two different ways to the same chair . . . But the chair is not in consciousness; not even as an image. What we find here is not

a semblance of the chair which suddenly worked its way into consciousness, . . . but a certain type of consciousness . . . which has a direct relation to the existing chair and whose very essence consists precisely of being related in this or that manner to the existing chair.

(PI: 4)

Imaging a chair, like seeing a chair, is being in a conscious state which has the chair as intentional object. It is not, says Sartre, a matter of being in a state whose intentional object is a 'semblance' of the chair. Indeed, he says that the 'expression "mental image [of x]" is confusing', and adds that it 'would be better to say "the imaginative consciousness of [x]"' (PI: 5), while accepting the impracticality of the reform. Ramming the point home, he goes on that

an image is nothing else than a relationship. The imaginative consciousness I have of Peter is not a consciousness of the image of Peter: Peter is directly reached; my attention is not directed on an image, but on an object.

(ibid.)

Care is in order here, since there are two ways in which one might image 'a chair'. One might image a previously encountered chair, such as one's favourite armchair. Or one might form an image of any old chair, having no particular one in mind. Only in the first sort of case does Sartre's talk of *the chair* figuring as intentional object seem defensible, since any appeal to such things as indefinite or unreal chairs is hardly illuminating (see the Appendix to Chapter 2). As we shall see, several further problems lurk hereabouts. But before coming to them, we need to ask what Sartre is after with his vehement insistence that imaging experiences do not have images as intentional objects.

## THE PICTURE GALLERY MODEL OF IMAGING

Sartre is opposing the view that visualising something involves having as intentional object a little picture of that thing, but a picture which happens to be in the mind rather than in public space (he calls this view 'the illusion of immanence' (PI: 2)). This Picture Gallery Model of Imaging involves at least three components. First, mental images are individual things, as a photograph is a piece of card. Second, there is an inner spectator or scanner to be aware of them. Ordinary visual awareness requires visual equipment, but in imaging a chair I do not use my eyes at all – they could be closed or removed first. So a mental analogue of eyes is needed if the inner picture is to be an object of visual awareness. Third, this then requires a distinction between the direct and the indirect objects of consciousness. For my image of the Eiffel Tower is still an image *of the Eiffel Tower*, rather than *of Happisburgh Lighthouse*. But if imaging is positing a mental picture, we have to say that the Eiffel Tower is only the indirect object of my consciousness, and that the mental picture itself is the direct object. Think of looking at a photograph of the Eiffel Tower. This is a way of having the tower as an object of consciousness, but it is natural to think of it as an indirect way, involving direct awareness of the photograph. (Sartre would not like this elucidation, as we shall see.)

It is predictable that Sartre should oppose this Picture Gallery model, given his conception of experience as activity-based rather than contemplative: since pictures, after all, are paradigmatic objects of contemplation. And in fact he objects convincingly to each of the above three components of it. As noted already, he considers consciousness to be empty, so that, in particular, he holds that it cannot contain pictures. He argues that it would be

> impossible to slip these material portraits into a conscious synthetic structure, without breaking the contacts, arresting the flow, breaking the continuity. Consciousness would cease being transparent to itself; its unity would be broken in every direction by unassimilable, opaque screens.
>
> (PI: 3–4)

This appeal to the Emptiness thesis is hardly perspicuous, but it is echoed by his objection to a version of the second component of the Picture Gallery Model of Imaging, the idea that consciousness contains an ego or self which is the spectator of the 'opaque screens'. Such an ego would, he says,

> be a hindrance. If it existed it would tear consciousness from itself; it would divide consciousness; it would slide into every consciousness like an opaque blade. [It] is the death of consciousness.
>
> (TE: 40)

In these passages, Sartre is in fact trying to reduce the Picture

Gallery Model to absurdity by taking it literally and showing how far it diverges in structure from what it is supposed to be a model of. He has two points in mind. Conscious experience is a flow of elements – thoughts, feelings, imagings – which succeed and overlap one another. But this flow is united in a synthesis, and is normally grasped and understood as a whole: 'imaginative consciousness is not given as a piece of wood which floats on the sea, but as a wave among waves' (PI: 14). Yet a gallery containing pictures and a spectator does not possess the necessary unity: it is, and remains, an unsynthesised collection of discrete items. Worse, some parts of the gallery would surely be occluded by the pictures hanging in front of them (or are the pictures see-through?). Others would sometimes lurk out of sight of the spectator (or has it got eyes in the back of its head? Can it see around things?). And this is all sheer nonsense. Sartre's second point invokes his claim that consciousness 'is all lightness, all translucence' (TE: 40). Now individuals such as tables and chairs, or photographs, are 'inexhaustible': they can be viewed from indefinitely many points of view (he says infinitely many – B&N: xxiii). So if there were pictures in consciousness, there would be a similar source of opacity within: it 'would be to refer to infinity the inventory which [consciousness] can make of itself' (B&N: xxvii). And this undermines the claim about special first-hand knowledge: our knowledge of our images and thoughts would be no more special than our knowledge of tables and chairs, and would be equally uncompletable. Since, however, the doctrine about the transparency of consciousness is controversial, this objection may not carry much weight. But this leaves the first: the idea that a unity or synthesis cannot be modelled on a three-dimensional space of discrete elements. And this seems correct. So given that the Picture Gallery Model of Imaging cannot be taken literally, it is useless as a model, and we should 'drop these spatial metaphors' (PI: 14). Note here that both parts of the Emptiness thesis are vindicated from a phenomenological point of view: neither representation nor ego is to be found in consciousness. This is another strand of Sartre's view that there is no self, that the mind is not a thing.

One may resist this because of a tendency to imagine the *spectator's* consciousness: could not it have a unified stream of consciousness which happened to be consciousness of mental pictures? This thought is encouraged, moreover, by Descartes' idea that the mind is an immaterial inhabitant of the body, and that the body cannot have mental characteristics. But this misses the point of the Picture Gallery proposal as attacked by Sartre. What he attacks is the proposal that the pictures (and the spectator) are *in the consciousness* of the imager. Descartes' view is the different one that the conscious imager is *in the head of the body* to which it is attached.[2] And this leaves the nature of imaging, and all other mental operations, still to be decided. Certainly, if any appeal is made to the idea of mental pictures, we can ask whether they are supposed to be in the immaterial ego or just in the associated brain. If the former, then the view involves the Picture Gallery Model of Imaging, and Sartre's criticism applies. There are further difficulties for other versions of the view, as we shall see in the following chapter. But for now it is enough to distinguish them from the Picture Gallery Model of Imaging, even if they ultimately collapse into it.

According to Sartre, further reflection on the phenomenology of imaging – concentration on what it is like actually to visualise – makes trouble for the third component of the Picture Gallery Model of Imaging, the indirect/direct object distinction. Sartre says that in the experience of imaging Peter,

> what my actual intention grasps is the corporeal Peter, the Peter I can see, touch, hear.
>
> (PI: 13)

My conscious attention is directed at Peter, not a picture of him, just as when I think about or see him. 'Peter is directly reached' (PI: 5), and it misrepresents the experience to claim otherwise. The temptation is to reply that, of course, imaging Peter is imaging *Peter*, and *not Patsie*. But this is accommodated, we may continue, by noting that Peter is the indirect object of consciousness, and we apparently remain free to speak also of a direct object. However, this again misses the point. Saying that the imaging has a picture as direct object has to mean that this is what attention is really focused on – why else use the word 'direct'? – even if the picture somehow puts one in mind of Peter rather than Patsie. And it is this claim about what attention is really focused on which is falsified, according to Sartre, by reflection on the experience. When I visualise him my conscious-ness is really, that is directly, focused on Peter, who is thus the act's intentional object. Again, Sartre's point seems well taken.

And as with the previous successful objection, Sartre's criticism turns on paying attention to the phenomenology, the 'what it is like', of the kind of experience in question.

## CRYPTO-OBJECTS

So far, so good. But surely imaging involves some kind of intermediary item, in the brain if nowhere else, and surely this is all that need be meant by the distinction between direct and indirect objects? Granted Sartre's successes against the Picture Gallery Model of Imaging, still there surely has to be *something* going on in my head when I image, and if my head is not empty, how can my consciousness be? So why not say that when, in imaging Peter, my consciousness is focused on him, and this act of consciousness involves an object of some kind which we may as well call the image of Peter? Let us designate such things *crypto-objects* ('crypto' = hidden, concealed).

It is not so easy to show that images must exist in the head or in consciousness. Presumably, when I just think about New York (rather than image it), things go on in my brain, without which I would not be able to think about New York at all. Even so, the thinking is still *about New York*: the brain's being involved hardly shows that the thinking is really or directly about it, and only indirectly about New York. Nor does it show that the brain activity is the crypto-object of the thinking, whatever that might mean. It merely shows that brain activity is a necessary condition of my thinking about New York. Similarly, then, the fact that my imaging Peter involves processes in the brain cannot show that these processes are any sort of object of the act, rather than simply a necessary condition of it.

True, but this is not the end of the matter. The residual problem is best approached via Sartre's account of using a real picture to bring something to mind. Suppose I want to visualise Peter, but cannot get a fix on him. I turn to a photograph, or similar *aide-mémoire*. At first I only see blotches of grey on a card. Then, suddenly, 'Peter appears' and I 'see him in' the photograph: now I am visualising him. It is very natural to call the photograph the direct object of my visualising, and Peter its indirect object. But, says Sartre, this is wrong. He says that we 'project' the interpretation on to such aids (PI: 30–1); that we become aware of *animating* the photograph, of lending it life, in order to make an image of it

(PI: 26)

that

in the imaginative attitude the picture is but a way in which Peter appears to me as absent

(PI: 25)

and that once this has happened

the picture is no longer an object, but operates as material for an image ... Everything I perceive enters into a projective synthesis which aims at the true Peter, a living being who is not present.

(PI: 23)

Sartre is urging that once my experience changes from seeing some blotches to visualising Peter, it is no longer true that the blotches are objects of my experience, direct or indirect, *even though I am still looking at them*. As far as the phenomenology is concerned, they have dropped out of contention, and my visual awareness is wholly focused on Peter. Peter now 'appears' to me (PI: 19). And up to a point, this is correct: phenomenologically, the aid melts away, and is no longer experienced as itself.

But care is needed. For however much the aid may drop out of my experience, and function as what Sartre calls *material* for imaging, I am still seeing it, even if I am no longer aware of doing so (cf. PI: 23). If someone set it alight or moved it, I should notice. Were I to close my eyes, my experience would change. So even though the aid is not a direct object of consciousness when I 'see Peter in it', it is still part of my experience. It is thus not at all misleading to refer to the aid as the crypto-object of the visualising, since it is implicated not merely as a necessary condition for the occurrence of the experience, as a brain process would be, but also at the phenomenological level. I see Peter as seated because that is how the photograph shows him. This is quite clearly what Sartre has in mind when speaking of transformed material.

Things get rather awkward for Sartre now, however, because he claims that ordinary cases of mental imaging have a similar structure, in that one has 'recourse to a certain material which acts as an analogue' of the imaged thing (PI: 17). There are, allegedly, differences. When I use an aid then the material can be perceived for itself . . . This photograph, taken by itself, is a thing.

(PI: 17; cf. 57ff.)

And Sartre denies that anything like this can be so in the case of mental imagery, since he denies that there are things in consciousness. Nevertheless, he remains committed to the idea of 'material' which is 'transformed' even in ordinary cases of mental imaging, and he thus seems also committed to the idea of a crypto-object. When I visualised Peter without an aid, still 'something loomed up which filled my intention' (PI: 18). But what is both sufficiently picture-like to do this, yet so unlike a picture that it is not a thing to be found in consciousness and seen with inner eyes? 'Here we meet with a great difficulty', says Sartre:

> In a word, we know . . . that in the mental image there is a psychic factor which functions as analogue but when we wish to ascertain more clearly the nature and components of this factor we are reduced to conjectures.
>
> (PI: 61)

Sartre's residual problem, then, is that of the crypto-object of an imaging experience: how can his commitment to this escape his own cogent objections to the Picture Gallery Model of Imaging?

But the reader may wonder why he lets himself get into this mess in the first place, after he has had the sense to reject the Picture Gallery Model of Imaging and to propose that imaging instead be thought of as simply a way of being conscious of an intentional object. Why drift back into talk of 'looming material', 'mental contents', 'psychic analogues' and all the rest? Why on earth lumber himself with crypto-objects?

## THE PROBLEM OF PHENOMENOLOGICAL PRESENCE

The problem springs from some hard-to-deny phenomenological facts about imaging (and we have seen the extent to which Sartre appeals to the phenomenology). Think first of the distinction between *seeing* a blackbird and *merely thinking about* one, without visualising it: one may either see that a blackbird is in the garden, or think (because you hear it) that one is. These two mental states differ in a number of respects, but one noteworthy difference is phenomenological. In seeing a blackbird, one has direct apprehension of shape, colour, texture, movement. One's consciousness is confronted by the blackbird and its visible properties: as Sartre puts it, the thing is 'encountered' (PI: 4; cf. 63ff.). Merely thinking (without seeing or visualising) is quite different. One may or may not also think about the colour, shape, movement of the blackbird. But one anyway does not experience them, and the blackbird is not encountered. Figuring as the intentional object of a thinking is thus phenomenologically quite different from figuring as the intentional object of a seeing. Let us say that in seeing, but not in thinking as such, the intentional objects of the state have *phenomenological presence*. Sartre mentions a related difference when he contrasts the way things are 'given' to perception and to thought (PI: 5–10). In perception a thing is presented to me from a point of view and in whatever guise the conditions dictate. I have to take it as it comes, and to see more of it I must take steps, whereupon it unfolds in a series of appearances as I walk around it, turn it over, etc. In thinking, though, I can consider a thing in its entirety: although I cannot see all the six sides of a cube together, I can certainly think of them all together.

Now one natural way to interpret all this is to note that perceived items just are 'there', available to the sense organs, whereas things merely thought about need not be. So, we might say, of course properties had by perceived things have a phenomenological presence not had by the properties of things merely thought about. Phenomenological presence just is availability to the senses. The brownness of this seen blackbird is affecting my sense organs in a way in which the blackness of her mate, which I believe to be next door and have not seen, is not (cf. B&N: 315ff.).

How does this bear on Sartre's problem with the crypto-objects of imaging? Well, he says that as far as the phenomenology is concerned, imaging

> seems to belong to perception. In the one, as in the other, the object presents itself in profiles, in projections.
>
> (PI: 7)

Later, he says that

> To form an image of Peter is to make an intentional synthesis which gathers up a mass of past events, which proclaims the identity of Peter by means of these diverse appearances and which presents this selfsame object in a certain form (in profile, three-quarters, full-length, half-length, etc.).
>
> (PI: 13)

Just as *being plump* and *being brown* can be phenomenologically present when I see a plump, brown blackbird, so they can be, it seems, when I image one: when I image a blackbird, shapes and colours are given as part of the experience, as they are when seeing. Whatever the differences between imaging and seeing – and Sartre catalogues several (e.g. PI: 5–16) – it is hard to deny this phenomenological similarity between them.[3] Unfortunately, Sartre also notes that one important difference between imaging and perceiving is that the first, but not the second, standardly takes place in the *absence* of the intentional object:

> The image . . . can posit the object as non-existent, or as absent, or as existing elsewhere; it can also . . . not posit its object as existing [i.e. involve suspension of judgement].
>
> (PI: 12)

And this ruins the above suggestion that phenomenological presence is to be explained in terms of availability to the sense organs. For once it is acknowledged that imaged intentional objects have the same kind of phenomenological presence as perceived ones, but without being perceptually present, that account of phenomenological presence is threatened. How can phenomenological presence be explained in terms of availability to the sense organs if there can be phenomenological presence when nothing need act on the senses, as in imaging?

It is now clear why the Picture Gallery Model of Imaging is so tempting. For if imaging is a sort of inner perception of pictures, then the account of phenomenological presence, in terms of availability to the senses, might be saved. Appropriate areas of a picture of a blackbird can themselves be brown, just like a seen blackbird, so if imaging involves some kind of inner sense, then we can say that such properties are available to the senses after all in imaging, and that that is what explains their phenomenological presence. It is equally clear why Sartre should be drawn into his problem with the crypto-object, even in the teeth of his own objections to the Picture Gallery Model. *The root of anyone's problem with imaging is the need to explain phenomenological presence.* If anything, the problem is exacerbated by arguments against the Picture Gallery Model.

One move now is to suggest that the phenomenology of imaging is parasitic on that of perception. The aim would be to avoid uncritical appeal to crypto-objects by showing that phenomenological presence is to be fundamentally explained in terms of availability to the senses, and that imaging is a derived or bastardised form of perception in which intentional objects enter in the phenomenological mode made available by perception. Of course, this has to be more than the merely psychological proposal that no one can image until the systems needed for veridical perception are up and running. Even the believer in mental pictures can accept this. It has to be, rather, the metaphysical proposal that imaging can only ever be understood as derived from veridical perception. Such a view is perhaps behind Sartre's mention of the 'paradox' that 'the imaginative consciousness aims at the Peter of Berlin through the [same] Peter who lived last year in Paris' (PI: 16), and his later claim that 'it is only what we know in some sort of way that we represent to ourselves as an image' (PI: 63). But whether or not he does intend to argue along these lines, we should note that there is anyway a deeper problem to face.

## THE ARGUMENT FROM ILLUSION

The astute reader will already have realised that the Problem of Phenomenological Presence makes trouble not merely for the special case of imaging, but for the matter of perception too. For one can certainly suffer visual hallucinations, where one seems to see a pink elephant when nothing is acting on the sense organs, and one can see something as round when it is really elliptical. In such cases, pinkness and roundness are phenomenologically present, even though there is no pink or round thing acting on the senses. It is thus not only in imaging that the absent or non-existent can figure as a phenomenologically present intentional object. And this suggests that it will not be enough to try to explain the phenomenological facts about imaging in terms of the phenomenological facts about perception. The Problem of Phenomenological Presence starts before we get to the special case of imaging.

The phenomenological presence of the non-existent or absent is one strand in the traditional Argument from Illusion, whose conclusion is that *all* experience, perceptual as well as that involved in imaging, requires phenomenologically present mental items as direct objects of experience.[4] Only in this way, the argument runs, can the phenomenology of perception and hallucination be accounted for. What this means, in the visual case, is that both seeing and imaging (and hallucinating) would be held to involve the direct awareness of mental pictures, the difference between them being that in seeing, but not in imaging (or hallucinating), the picture is appropriately caused by items in the immediate surroundings. Misperception is explained in terms of mismatch between the mental picture and what it is a picture of (the indirectly perceived individual), and hallucination regarded as the enjoying of a mental picture brought about by non-standard causes, such as drink or drugs. Traditionally, as remarked in Chapter 1, the mental pictures are known as *ideas* or *representations*, and the theory of perception resulting from this approach is known as *indirect realism*. And this approach seems to require an extended gallery model – what we shall call the Picture Gallery Model of Visual Experience. Whether or not the view amounts to Descartes' claim that the mind is an immaterial substance depends, in effect, on what the inner spectator is made of, and it is not immediately ruled out that some attempts at this model might be materialistic, positing image-like structures in the brain and a material scanner.

All of this, of course, comes into sharp conflict with Sartre's activity-based model of conscious mental life, as well as with his specific objections to the Picture Gallery Model of Imaging. But it has emerged that the key issue – that of phenomenological presence – concerns the general theory of experience and perception, rather than simply the restricted domain of mental imaging. At this point, then, we shall leave the topic of imaging, and turn to the theory of perception.

## NOTES AND FURTHER READING

1  Joseph Conrad, *Heart of Darkness* (London: Dent, 1974): 48.
2  Since the Cartesian ego is supposed to have no spatial characteristics, it can be argued that it is not really in the head, even though that is where it is supposed to interact with the body. But even if this makes sense, the point is quite trivial, and there seems nothing wrong with the idea that the ego should be situated at a point in space, even if it is unextended.
3  There is quite a large psychological literature concerned with how similar, in fact, imaging and perceiving are. See, for example, *Imagery* ed. N. Block (Cambridge, Mass.: MIT Press, 1981).
4  This style of argument is employed in Descartes' *Meditations*. For a clear account of the Argument from Illusion see J. Dancy, *Introduction to Contemporary Epistemology* (Oxford: Blackwell, 1985): 153ff. and index.

# Chapter 6

# Realism and idealism

I have heard the key
Turn in the door once and turn once only
We think of the key, each in his prison
Thinking of the key, each confirms a prison

T.S. Eliot[1]

Perception is a mind–world relationship *par excellence*. Sartre's views on it, then, are bound up with his views about the relationships between Being In-itself and Being For-itself. And here we collide with a number of traditional concerns. Philosophy had been focused on the relations between mind and body, especially the one between the knower and the known, ever since Descartes. Philosophical accounts of the material world were standardly embedded in theories of how the mind encounters it. (One recent trend assumes the reverse strategy: theory of knowledge is 'naturalised', or seen in the light of the deliverances, real or hoped for, of natural science.)[2] But in addition to this, although Sartre was neither the first to embrace the doctrine of intentionality, nor the first to urge an activity-based model of conscious mental life, his was, arguably, the first reasonably clear attempt to assess the combination in traditional philosophical terms, and this too requires an investigation into mind–world relationships. But what this investigation yields, he concludes, is a view which is *neither realist nor idealist*. And there is a problem here. For idealism is the view that the world is dependent for its existence on minds, and realism is the view that it is not. And how can there be any middle ground? Surely either the material world depends upon minds for its existence, or it does not.[3] This is the issue we must now face, entwined as it is with the Problem of Phenomenological Presence in the theory of perception.

## DESCARTES AND BERKELEY

Here is the situation as Sartre saw it. Intentional objects are the things we can be conscious of, which make mental states what they are. But this suggests that intentional objects are mental entities, especially if the Picture Gallery Model of Visual Experience is in the background.[4] When I have a hallucination of a red triangle, the thought goes, my intentional objects include the properties *being red* and *being triangular*, as had *by my idea or inner picture*. Even when I see a red triangle, the thought goes on, the direct objects of my experience are still the properties of the idea even if, this time, it is caused by an 'external' red triangle (the indirect object). This is what Sartre calls *realism*: the view that the material world is 'external', that is, exists outside or independently of the mind, which gets to know about it indirectly through its effects (ideas). Sartre here usually mentions Descartes' view that immaterial mind and material world exist independently of one another: the mind has its nature, which consists in having ideas, and the material world has its, which consists in occupying space. Descartes actually considered mind and world to interact causally, and so not to be completely independent. But this is irrelevant, since it leaves intact the idea that immaterial minds and material bodies have independent modes of being, and so *could be* separated. Moreover, this interactionism easily transmutes into parallelism, the view that mind and body are as Descartes said except that they do not interact, but are preset (e.g. by God) to run concurrently. Parallelists keep the main planks of Descartes' position, and avoid its biggest problem – how is interaction possible? – by denying that it occurs. The picture remains of mind existing here, and the material world existing 'out there'.[5]

Let us call subscribers to this two-way independence of mind and material world *Cartesian realists*. According to Cartesian realists, both of the following are true:

1 The world could exist without any minds in it.
2 Minds could exist without any surrounding material world or environment.

Importantly, the idea has materialistic versions. For example, some forms of the view that the mind is the brain entail that an atom-for-atom replica of my brain, kept from the start in a vat of nutrients and fed the right inputs from a computer, embodies a thinking subject psychologically the same as me.[6] This is material-istic Cartesian realism: the mind is in here, existing in virtue of brain activity, the world is out there, surrounding the vat or skull. Again, *de facto* interaction does not affect the in-principle inde-pendence. Nor does the fact that brains are *part* of the material world. For it remains that the mind/brain enjoys one mode of being, and the (rest of) the material world enjoys another. Mind and world could be separated in principle: and this two-way independence is the heart of Cartesian realism.

As we have already noted, Sartre explicitly rejects Descartes: he repudiates ideas, and denies that the mind is a thing or substance (he calls this 'Descartes' substantialist illusion', (B&N: 84)). This, of course, rules out materialistic Cartesian realism too. He con-cludes that

the being of the phenomenon can on no account act upon consciousness. In this way we have ruled out a *realistic* con-ception of the relations of the phenomenon with consciousness.
(B&N: xl; cf. 171)

Consciousness cannot receive any effects of the world (such as ideas): there are no such effects, the mind is not a *thing* which can receive them.

Before turning to the arguments that Sartre gives for this repudi-ation, we should note that Cartesian realism anyway suffers from severe epistemological difficulties. How could I know whether there are any 'external' things if all I encounter are ideas? Descartes put the assault on this issue at the centre of his philosophy, but his indifferent success encouraged views on which 'external' things are ruled out altogether. (Recall again Brentano's claim, at the begin-ning of Chapter 2, that by *intentional object* he '[does] not mean a reality'.) Thus Berkeley, who thought the very idea of material things not directly accessible to the mind to be incoherent, even though he retained Descartes' view that the mind exists by having ideas. What results is *Berkeleyan idealism*, the view that the world is a community of minds, and that material things are really col-lections of ideas.[7] Berkeley's universe is Descartes' universe minus the 'external' material world. Berkeleyan idealism drops claim (1) of Cartesian realism but retains claim (2). Now, Sartre's rejection of aspects of Descartes' system retained by Berkeley – ideas, mind-as-substance – commit him to a rejection of Berkeleyan idealism too. But for good measure he attacks in detail Berkeley's dictum *esse est percipi* ('to be is to be perceived') in the course of giving his own account (see the following chapter).

Hence it is clear and uncontroversial that Sartre is *neither a (Cartesian) realist nor a (Berkeleyan) idealist*. But this leaves two related problems. First, there are other forms of idealism besides Berkeley's. Kant attacks Berkeley, yet his view is called *transcendental idealism*, since it entails that the perceptible world (the world of material things, causes and effects) is mind dependent. Kant does not hold that material things are collections of ideas, but he agrees with Berkeley that they cannot exist without minds. He distinguishes the knowable phenomenal world of familiar things from the unknowable noumenal world of things-in-themselves, and holds that the phenomenal world only exists because of, roughly, an interaction between the mind and the noumenal. So without minds there would be, at most, the noumenal world. There would be no familiar perceptible things.[8]

Nothing said so far is incompatible with Sartre's being a transcendental idealist. True, he claims to be neither realist nor idealist, but given the way we defined these terms above there is no evident middle ground: either the material world depends for its existence on the mind or it does not. True, too, Sartre explicitly follows Husserl in rejecting the Kantian noumenon, as we shall see. But it is not always clear how much of Husserl Sartre accepts, and Husserl aims to be a form of transcendental idealist who dispenses with the noumenon:

> The attempt to conceive the universe of true being as something lying outside the universe of possible consciousness, possible knowledge, possible experience . . . is nonsensical.[9]

Relatedly, then, we still need to find out what Sartre's view is. We shall see in the following chapter that he is best seen as a form of (non-Cartesian) *realist*: when he denies realism, he is really only denying Cartesian realism. The question of his leanings towards transcendental idealism is also discussed there. But before getting to all that, we first have to clear the ground by seeing just why Sartre rejects the view of mind essentially shared by both Cartesian realists and Berkeleyan idealists.

## THEORIES OF PERCEPTION

Given our focus on experience, it is legitimate to make the issue more manageable by concentrating on the theory of perception. Then we can cast Descartes and Berkeley, not too unfairly, as *indirect realist* and *phenomenalist* respectively. According to indirect realists, perception of material things is mediated by our ideas or sense data or visual representations of them, of which we are directly aware. According to the phenomenalist, perception *consists in* having the sense data: there is no mediation, because there are no 'external', mind-independent things. The other standard approach to perception is *direct (or naive) realism*. Proponents of this accept the phenomenalist claim that perception is not mediated, but also accept the indirect realist view that perceiving involves a relation to independent material things (i.e. things which can exist even if there are no minds). According to direct realists, there really are independent material things, but our perception of them is unmediated by awareness of ideas or representations. Somehow the perceiving consciousness is open to material things (which are thus not 'external', even though they can exist without being perceived). To put it too crudely, whereas Berkeley takes over Descartes' universe but omits the 'external' material things, leaving only the minds and their ideas, the direct realist takes it over but omits the ideas, leaving the minds (or better, human persons) and independent (but no longer 'external') things.[10] For present purposes, we can see indirect realist and phenomenalist as making common cause against the direct realist, since the first two both believe in ideas or visual representations, and the last does not. As remarked, Descartes and Berkeley essentially share the same model of the mind: their dispute is over what lies 'outside'.

Clearly then, first: since Sartre rejects both Cartesian realism and Berkeleyan idealism, he has to be a direct realist in perception by default. If he thinks we perceive material things, and denies that mediating entities exist, what other alternative is there? He says

> Perception is articulated only on the ontological foundation of presence to the world, and the world is revealed concretely as the ground of each individual perception.
>
> (B&N: 181)

That looks like direct realism: the mind (*qua* perceiver) exists not by having ideas but by being present to the world. Later, he goes on

> We shall best account for the original phenomenon of per-
> ception by insisting on the fact that the relation of the quality
> [i.e. perceived property such as colour] to us is that of absolute
> proximity (it *'is there'*, it haunts us) . . . but we must add that this
> proximity implies a distance. It is what is immediately out of
> reach, what by definition refers us to ourselves as an emptiness
> . . . [i.e. it is] not a subjective impression.
>
> (B&N: 187)

Saying that Sartre is a direct realist does not necessarily prejudge the question whether he is a transcendental idealist. Kant was quite happy with *empirical realism*, the view that material things are not collections of ideas, but somehow objective. And it is not obvious that a position such as Kant's *has to* involve the claim that perception of such objects is mediated by awareness of ideas. If so, then Sartre could be a direct realist in perception, in the sense of *direct empirical realist*, yet still subscribe to a form of transcendental idealism. So this question has not been begged.

However, we have conveniently narrowed down the dispute between Sartre and Descartes/Berkeley to the issue of ideas or visual representations. Now we saw in the previous chapter why one can seem to be forced into accepting them – the Argument from Illusion, the Problem of Phenomenological Presence – but we also saw the force of Sartre's objections to Picture Gallery models of the mind. So we need first to see how these arguments can be generalised to see off indirect realism and phenomenalism, Descartes and Berkeley. Then we need to see (in the following chapter) how Sartre might cope with the Problem of Phenomenological Presence.

## WHAT EXPERIENCE IS LIKE

The curious thing is that while ideas are posited in the theory of perception under pressure from the phenomenological facts, the usual accounts of them are phenomenologically ludicrous. The first problem is that the move seems to force a restriction of attention to limited aspects of the visual scene (shapes, colours) when discussing its phenomenology. And this is because it tends to bring with it, as we have seen, the view that visual consciousness involves the inner perception of picture-like entities. For although even ordinary pictures can be 'of' worldly items like tables and chairs, they are things in their own right, with their own intrinsic features, not the least of which are various shaped patches of colour. In so far as picture-like things occur in the head, then, it is natural, if not obligatory, to take them too as having similar properties drawn from the same limited stock. Then given the ordinary, dictionary definition of a phenomenon as 'that of which a sense or the mind takes immediate note', colours and shapes are all the visual phenomenology one could expect to see mentioned by those in the Descartes/Berkeley camp. Imagine confronting a huge picture of Marvin Hagler. To the knowledgeable viewer this could seem like visually confronting Hagler himself. But despite what is right in Sartre's claim that in 'seeing Hagler in' the picture one's experience would no longer have the picture as an intentional object, nevertheless, there is a sense in which all that the viewer *sees* is the colour mosaic on the canvas. For this is what acts on his or her eyes. Then the point about the Picture Gallery Model of Visual Experience is that all we are *ever* really visually aware of, according to it, are colour mosaics. As far as visual awareness goes, we are permanently in the position of viewers in an inner gallery. Hence it is supposed that the phenomenologically given, where vision is concerned, consists of a colour mosaic. Just as the viewer in the real gallery is really seeing a colour mosaic, even if it is 'transformed' so that the viewer is in a sense visually aware of Marvin Hagler, so each of us, given the Picture Gallery Model of Visual Experience, is really visually confronted by shapes and colours, and nothing more, whenever we enjoy visual experience. Similarly, just as the viewer might turn attention on the picture, and see it explicitly as a colour mosaic, so each of us, on the Picture Gallery model, can introspect, or reflect on the nature of visual experience in itself, and become explicitly aware of its austere phenomenological basis.

Sartre, we know, rejects this austere conception of the phenomenological and instead considers that the objects of awareness are intentional objects such as blackbirds and streetcars, and not little mental pictures of them. And he is quite right. To see this, note first that a difficult question arises concerning how our rich visual conception of the surrounding world relates to the colours and shapes which are all that we are allegedly given in visual awareness. We do not ordinarily speak of the visual scene in austere terms. We speak of seeing blackbirds, seeing that it is a steep walk home, seeing that Maisie is unhappy and so on. Our usual ways of saying what we see are at odds with the austere account of the phenomenological, and in accordance with Sartre's activity-based conception. The traditional reply is that we construct or infer our rich conception of the visual scene from the austere phenomenological base, just as viewers of real pictures learn to see them *as* pictures rather than as colour mosaics.[11] What we 'really' see is a patch of dappled brown, and we then feed in extra material, perhaps on the basis of previous experience, and claim to 'see a blackbird'. 'Seeing', in this last, ordinary-language sense, is thus alleged to go beyond visual phenomenology, analogous to the way in which the viewer's 'That's Hagler!', on seeing the real picture mentioned above, goes beyond what is actually seen.

This manoeuvre can be overturned by simple attention to what one's own visual experience is actually like, as recommended by Sartre and the Phenomenologists.[12] Because talk of what is 'given' or phenomenologically available just is talk of what consciousness is like, of how the world is presented to us, there can be no other way of assessing it. And it is clear that the world is not visually given to us as a colour mosaic. Our rich descriptions of what we see are faithful reflections of how the world visually appears to us, and they are not the result of putting constructions on an austere phenomenology. The basic Sartrean idea that our consciousness is open to the world is confirmable by simple reflection on what one's own experience is like. Try it now. One can learn, of course, to focus on the shapes and colours in the visual scene: to concentrate on how things appear, and see that the round plate actually presents an elliptical aspect, that the brown table in fact appears to be striped with white due to reflected light, and so on.[13] But this is not the sort of aspect switch that is involved when the viewer stops 'seeing Hagler in' the picture, and instead sees it as a flat painted area. Nor is it 'introspection' if that is thought of as a kind of looking inwards. For when I attend to the actual appearances presented by the plate or table, my experiences still have *the plate* and *the table* as intentional objects. It is by concentrating more carefully on the plate that I come to appreciate the elliptical appearance it is presenting: I do not switch attention from the plate to something else, more directly confronted by my mind's eye, and see that it is elliptical. Reflection on the character of visual experience is as world-directed as seeing itself. Contrast the viewer in the gallery: in desisting from 'seeing Hagler in' a picture, and concentrating on the paint, attention *does* switch from one item to another. It is not that one remains visually aware of Hagler, but comes to see him as smeared with brown paint.

It is true, as findings in the physiology of perception indicate, that we in some sense 'construct' our conception of the world on the basis of meagre sensory input. Light and other energy originates in the surrounding world and activates our surfaces, and messages work along the nerves to the brain, where transformations of the input occur. Somehow all of this adds up to our experience of the world. And in this sense, all we are 'given' are aggravated nerve endings: other components of the experiential mixture are inside already. Now this account of the physiology has much the same formal structure as the Picture Gallery model, according to which we are given shapes and colours (where sight is concerned) on the basis of which we construct or infer our rich characterisations of what we see. In each case there is alleged to be a thin input which is beefed up by internal processing. Despite this similarity of formal structure, however, there is no good argument from physiology to the Picture Gallery model. First, from the fact that my body is 'given' certain stimulations, it does not follow that these stimulations are phenomenologically given, i.e. are what I am immediately conscious of. If, as Sartre claims, consciousness is a way of being related to the surrounding world, then it is this which is given, and which helps to constitute the phenomenology. The fact that this interaction with the surroundings is underpinned by complex physical processes cannot itself show that experience is phenomenologically more austere than it seems to be, or that really one is aware of some limited range of these underlying processes. Recall again the point about thinking of New York. The fact that this too is underwritten by complex brain processes does not show that such thinking is really about the brain, or that these brain processes are themselves somehow given to the conscious mind. Second, from the fact that the information input to the senses is processed by my brain, it does not follow that *I* perform inferences or constructions in coming to have visual experience: or not consciously, anyway. Say, if you like, that the brain processing is a form of unconscious construction. But that emphasises very nicely that we are no longer talking about phenomenology (what consciously goes on). There is a great deal going on in my brain which is necessary for me to operate. If this makes you want to say that I am unconsciously set on, say, keeping my heart beating, making my fingernails grow and digesting my breakfast, then that is one thing. But this is clearly no contribution to the subject of phenomenology, is no part of a description of what it is like to be me (cf. B&N: 312ff.).

Nor is phenomenological absurdity the only problem that the Picture Gallery Model of Visual Experience suffers from. To introduce these further problems, we should first consider what is called 'the homunculus problem' in recent psychology and cognitive science. In virtue of what is my inner spectator conscious of the mental pictures? Does it need a spectator too, which would need a spectator, which . . .? (cf. B&N: 321). Or is my spectator visually conscious in another way? But if so, why cannot I be visually conscious in that way too, thereby dispensing with the spectator?[14] Now this may not seem too devastating on reflection. For one can reply that the Problem of Phenomenological Presence gives an independent reason to believe in inner pictures, and hence gives a reason why *I* cannot be visually conscious without a spectator in my head. This leaves the visual consciousness of the spectator a mystery. But if the proponents of the view, materialist or immaterialist, can account for this without falling into regress, then the mystery would only be temporary. Crucial here would be the thought that the spectator could not be prey to misperception or hallucination. If this matter could be settled satisfactorily, and a regress avoided, then real progress would have been made. Nevertheless, there are insuperable obstacles for both materialists and immaterialists who attempt this, in addition to the foregoing phenomenological problem with their view.

First, if it is said that the pictures and their spectator are in consciousness, then there are Sartre's convincing objections based on the unity of consciousness (Chapter 5). Second, it is impossible for pictures, which occupy space, to be contained in an immaterial substance, which is supposed not to be extended in space (this is a problem for immaterialists). Third, we do not expect to find coloured pictures in the skull, which is full of grey matter and dark inside (this is the corresponding problem for the materialist, or for immaterialists who say that the spectator scans material structures in the brain).

For the foregoing reasons, then, the Picture Gallery Model of

Visual Experience cannot be sustained. This means that the fate of the Descartes/Berkeley model of the mind, and hence of the alternatives to direct realism in perception, hangs on whether the phenomenological presence of properties in an experience can be explained in terms of a mediating item other than an inner picture, such as a brain state or other condition of the optic system. And this thought is barely intelligible, given that, as we have seen, visual experience 'goes right up to' the world of visible things. For what is required is some intermediate item which somehow constitutes, by being given to consciousness, the phenomenology of (say) being visually presented with a blackbird, in all its openness-to-the-world. And it is very hard to see what could be sufficiently blackbirdish save an image or picture of a blackbird, interpreted as such. But this is no use, as we have been seeing. It is certainly no good, as cognitive scientists tend to do, to speak vaguely of brain structures and the like which have certain formal picture-like properties. If the brain structures are to do the present phenomenological job, they evidently have to *be* pictures.

There is a tendency to underestimate this problem, due to the slippery term 'sensation'. Construed ordinarily, a sensation is a putative bodily occurrence available to consciousness: examples are pains or tickles. Sensations are phenomenologically present, but are also constituted by bodily goings-on – or at least, they will have to be if materialism is true. So unless the existence of pains demonstrates immaterialism, some aspects of phenomenology have to be grounded in brain or nerve activity. So if some, why not all? Why not apply whatever account can be given of the phenomenology of pains to the case of visual perception? Thus, one sees talk of such things as 'sensations of yellow', which we are alleged to have when we see things as yellow, and which are supposed to constitute the phenomenology of the state of seeing (or seeming to see) something as yellow. If pains are bodily occurrences, but still phenomenologically present, why cannot sensations of yellow, also phenomenologically present, yet be bodily occurrences, brain activity or the like?

But the phrase 'sensation of yellow' is a 'pure daydream of the psychologist' (B&N: 315). It is supposed to be relevant to the phenomenology of vision, and is modelled on the idea of phenomenologically present bodily occurrences such as pains and tingles. But nothing is experienced in a bodily way in standard visual perception. Seeing a ripe lemon in good light involves the property of *being yellow* as phenomenologically present. But this, unlike a pain or tickle, is not experienced as a state of or occurrence in the body (cf. B&N: 311). Indeed, absolutely nothing at all is, usually. What is experienced strikes one as a state of the material world: yellowness, as phenomenologically encountered, no more strikes one as a state of the body than does lemonhood. Thus Sartre:

> Too often quality [i.e. a perceptible property] has been conceived as a simple subjective determination, and its quality-of-being has then been confused with the subjectivity of the psychic. The problem has then appeared to be especially to explain the constitution of an object-pole conceived as the transcendent unity of the qualities . . . [But a] quality does not objectivate itself if it is subjective.
>
> (B&N: 186)

One can experience sensations in the visual apparatus, of course. Looking at the sun can cause dazzling, smarting eyes and so on. But this is not normal visual experience and, if anything, mention of it underlines the disanalogies between sensation and visual perception. Seeing the pale yellow sun through thin cloud does not contain any phenomenological component analogous to the sharp sensations felt in the eyes when it is viewed at midday in a clear sky.[15]

In sum, the prospects for the Descartes/Berkeley model of the mind, and its attendant theories of perception (indirect realism and phenomenalism respectively) are much worse than its proponents assume. Either the view sinks back into the untenable Picture Gallery Model of Visual Experience, or it is simply never explained, or even sketched, how phenomenological presence is otherwise to be accommodated. Stripped of the incoherent talk of 'sensations of yellow' and the like, Cartesianism without inner pictures is a dogma devoid of phenomenological substance. And with the inner pictures it is manifestly phenomenologically absurd.

So what are the prospects for Sartre's direct realism?

## NOTES AND FURTHER READING

1   T.S. Eliot, 'The Waste Land', *The Complete Poems and Plays of T.S. Eliot* (London: Faber & Faber, 1969).
2   For the idea of 'naturalised' epistemology, see W.V. Quine's 'Epistemology naturalized' in his *Ontological Relativity and Other Essays* (New

York: Columbia University Press, 1969), and P. Churchland's *Scientific Realism and the Plasticity of Mind* (Cambridge: Cambridge University Press, 1979). For trenchant criticism see H. Putnam, *Realism and Reason* (Cambridge: Cambridge University Press, 1983) chs. 11–13.

3  For realism and idealism, see T. Sprigge, *Theories of Existence* (Harmondsworth: Penguin, 1985) and J. Heal, *Fact and Meaning* (Oxford: Blackwell, 1989) ch. 2.

4  Other reasons for supposing that intentional objects must be mental are discussed in D.W. Smith and R. MacIntyre, *Husserl and Intentionality* (Dordrecht: Reidel, 1982) ch. 2.

5  For Descartes' rather limp musings on mind–body interaction see, for example, the letters to Princess Elizabeth in *Descartes: Philosophical Writings* tr. G.E.M. Anscombe and P.T. Geach (London: Nelson, 1954). For parallelism see T. Honderich, *A Theory of Determinism* (Oxford: Oxford University Press, 1988): 111–12

6  For different varieties of the view that the mind is the brain see P. Carruthers, *Introducing Persons* (London: Croom Helm, 1986) ch. 5. For the brain in a vat see H. Putnam, *Reason, Truth and History* (Cambridge: Cambridge University Press, 1981) ch. 1.

7  See G. Berkeley, *Treatise Concerning the Principles of Human Knowledge* in M. R. Ayers ed. *Berkeley: Philosophical Works* (London: Dent, 1975).

8  See I. Kant, *Critique of Pure Reason* tr. N. Kemp Smith (London: Macmillan, 1933) 'Transcendental Analytic', ch. III.

9  See E. Husserl, *Cartesian Meditations* tr. D. Cairns (Dordrecht: Kluwer, 1950): 84.

10  See J. Dancy, *Introduction to Contemporary Epistemology* (Oxford: Blackwell, 1985) chs. 10 and 11.

11  For the classical empiricist account of how our rich phenomenological characterisations are related to what is strictly 'given', see G. Berkeley, *An Essay Towards a New Theory of Vision* in M. R. Ayers, *Berkeley.*

12  According to Husserl, strict philosophical reflection on the nature of experience involves an *'epoché'*, that is a withdrawal from the world-directed attitude we normally have when enjoying experience. Under the *epoché*, we 'bracket' belief in the worldly objects of experience, and concentrate attention on the experiences themselves. One thus arrives at a conception of what the experiences are like independently of belief in the world: see the First Meditation in Husserl, *Cartesian Meditations*. Husserl rightly points out (32–5) that this procedure does not deliver what we are calling the austere conception of the phenomenological. Nevertheless, he tends to slide from the innocent thesis about switching attitudes to the very different and strikingly Cartesian claim that under the *epoché* one gains a conception of what experiences are like *whether or not they have worldly objects*. But bracketing *belief in* the world is not at all the same thing as bracketing *the world*: perhaps experiences *have to have* worldly objects even though we can suspend judgement on whether they do. The same mistake is rife in the commentaries and in the analytical tradition: see, for example, H. Putnam, *Reason, Truth and History*: 28–9. Sartre, it should be stressed, is innocent of it.

13  For a seminal account of what reflection on how things actually

appear delivers, and what is supposed to follow from this, see B. Russell, *The Problems of Philosophy* (Oxford: Oxford University Press, 1967) ch. 1.

14   For the homunculus problem see, for example, N. Block, 'Mental pictures and cognitive science' reprinted in W. Lycan ed. *Mind and Cognition* (Oxford: Blackwell, 1989): 590–4.

15   A rather more subtle version of this view is suggested by Jonathan Dancy, *Contemporary Epistemology.* The problem is to account for the phenomenology of perceptual states. Dancy proposes that we

> opt for a mixed theory of perception, under which perception is some sort of combination of 'sensation' and belief.
>
> (172)

But he does not conceive of the 'sensory' element of a perceptual state as something which can be detached from the belief element and just enjoyed on its own:

> Instead of taking perception to be a combination of two separable elements, sensory and cognitive, we should take perception to be a characteristic *form* of belief (or of a tendency to believe), one not sharable by those who lack the relevant sensory input, and one where the tendency to believe is not separable from the occurrence of that input.
>
> (ibid.)

But this very subtlety masks a major weakness in the suggestion. If the 'sensory' element is in this way supposed to be undetachable from the rest of the experience, then the very use of the word 'sensation' is suspect. Real sensations, after all, *are* detachable elements of experience: I can, for instance, detach the sensation of pain itself from my troubled awareness that my leg hurts, or the tingles under my arms from my general sense of unease. If the alleged 'sensory' elements of a perceptual state are not in this way detachable, why speak of 'sensations' at all? If we are told that these alleged perceptual sensations are of a very special kind, phenomenologically quite unlike real sensations in that they cannot be detached and scrutinised separately, it is evident that we are being cheated. 'Special' sensory elements, 'characteristic *forms* of belief' (to use Dancy's phrase), are just new labels for the fact that perception involves phenomenological reality: there is no *model* of this on offer, given the breakdown in the analogy with real sensations.

# Chapter 7

# Sartrean realism

I met the Universe in books: assimilated, classified, labelled and studied, but still impressive; and I confused the chaos of my experiences through books with the hazardous course of real events. Hence my idealism which it took me thirty years to undo.

Sartre[1]

Sartre develops his alternative to Descartes and Berkeley in the course of shaping up to a nasty problem which he detects in Husserl's transcendental-idealism-without-noumena (Chapter 6). First, if minds have no contents, what is their way of existing? A Cartesian ego exists by having ideas. A brain exists in virtue of its material structure. Neither view can help Sartre. Second, if appearances are not ideas in the mind, yet at the same time have no noumenal support, what is *their* way of existing? Sartre links this to the thought that the appearance/reality dualism has been replaced in Husserl's scheme by another – finite/infinite:

> Does this mean that by reducing the existent to its manifestations we have succeeded in overcoming *all* dualisms [of the phenomenal/noumenal type]? It seems rather that we have converted them all into a new dualism: that of finite and infinite . . . a certain 'potency' returns to inhabit the phenomenon and confer on it its very transcendence – a potency to be developed in a series of real or possible appearances.

(B&N: xxii–xxiii)

We think not only that the being of a perceived thing goes beyond our perception of it, but also that there is no end to the ways in which it can be perceived (by different perceivers, from different perspectives, at different times . . . – cf. B&N: xxiii). But what, he asks, sustains the infinity of appearances which this table is?:

> there arises a legitimate problem concerning the being of this appearing.

> (B&N: xxiv)

Combining the two questions – how do minds exist if they do not have contents and how do appearances exist if they are not supported by noumena? – it is evident that there is a danger of incoherent circularity. One might suggest that the mind exists by apprehending appearances, and so is dependent on apprehended things for its existence. But then one might *also* suggest that appearances, lacking noumenal support, exist by being apprehended. Yet surely something has to 'come first'? Either the mind has an independent mode of being that enables it to sustain appearance, or vice versa. Otherwise,

> the totality 'perceived-perception' lacks the support of a solid being.

> (B&N: xxvi)

Sartre seems to believe that Husserl's transcendental idealism is trapped in this incoherent circle, and he sees his task as one of getting out without falling into Cartesian realism or other forms of idealism. In outline, he argues that Being For-itself and Being In-itself, though inextricably inter-related, nevertheless have distinctive principles of being of their own. This is the point of his attack on Berkeley's *esse est percipi*. First, he argues that the being of consciousness could not consist in being perceived; second, that nor could the being of appearance.

## THE BEING OF CONSCIOUSNESS

He begins with:

> an idealism intent on reducing being to the knowledge which we have of it, ought first to give some kind of guarantee for the being of knowledge . . . Thus the being of knowledge can not be measured by knowledge.

> (B&N: xxvi–xxvii)

If consciousness is to support the existence of appearance, as idealists intend, then it must itself have some kind of independent being, which must consist in more than being perceived.

Sartre obviously cannot here invoke the material or immaterial substantial self, existing not by being perceived but by having ideas. But why not say that consciousness exists *by perceiving*? This, after all, is close to Husserl's view, at the centre of Sartre's philosophy, that all consciousness is consciousness *of* something. Why should not the *esse* of consciousness consist in being directed at intentional objects? (cf. B&N: xxvii–xxviii). Sartre replies that consciousness, even though it is always directed at an intentional object, must also be self-consciousness, because otherwise we shall be unable to avoid the 'absurd' consequence of 'a consciousness which is ignorant of itself, an unconscious' (B&N: xxviii).

This is dubitable. Some non-human animals appear to be conscious of their surroundings though lacking in self-consciousness. Sartre might respond with Descartes' contentious idea that non-human animals are non-conscious natural machines (cf. B&N: 224). However, even humans sometimes appear to be conscious of things without being conscious of that fact. I may drive along in a daydream, avoiding the obstacles of which I must thus be conscious, but absorbed in thoughts about Sartre. This may not be a wholly convincing example, since I remain able to snap out of my reverie and attend to my awareness of the traffic if prompted. That I might not afterwards *remember* being conscious of trucks and police officers does not show that I was not implicitly aware of being aware of them, and the fact that I could have been prompted in the appropriate way at the time rather suggests that I was. It is relevant to note here that in Sartre's view, to be self-conscious is to be able to bring the nature of one's awareness to mind:

> If anyone . . . should ask, 'What are you doing there?' I should reply at once, 'I am counting'. This reply aims not only at the instantaneous consciousness which I can achieve by reflection but at those fleeting consciousnesses which have passed without being reflected-on in my immediate past.
>
> (B&N: xxix; cf. TE: 89)

But perhaps there are other examples of what we want – human consciousness which is not self-consciousness. One example is that if X looks sexually aroused to Y, it may be because X's lips are red and pupils dilated, even though Y may not be conscious of picking up this information, even on reflection. So Y must in some sense be conscious of those red lips etc., even though he or she may remain unaware of this, even if prompted.[2]

This casts doubt on Sartre's assertion that non-self-conscious consciousness is 'absurd'. But perhaps he should make a weaker claim. Whatever we say about consciousness as such, the kind of consciousness *we* enjoy is open to reflection to a very high degree. Examples like the bases of sexy looks aside, a lot of my ongoing conscious experience is at least capable of being scrutinised by me. It is not true that *typical human consciousness* consists merely in directedness at objects.

So why not say that to be self-conscious in our way is to be able to take our own conscious acts as intentional objects, or direct our consciousness at itself as well as at our material surroundings? Now Sartre agrees that we can reflect like this on our own conscious activity (B&N: xxix; STE: 56; PI: 1; TE: 43ff.). Yet as we have already seen, he denies that this is the only form of self-consciousness. To suppose it is, he claims, is either to start off a regress, which is 'absurd', or to posit an arbitrary stopping point where once again unconsciousness intrudes (B&N: xxviii–xxix). If we say that Act 1's self-awareness consists in its being the (potential) object of Act 2, then either Act 2 will be left as not itself a (potential) object of consciousness, or we will need to posit Act 3, then Act 4 and so on.

This is hardly knock-down. What is wrong with the thought that we have a capacity to reflect which, although limited in practice, is unbounded in principle? Nevertheless, Sartre is right to the extent that although we have a seemingly open-ended capacity to reflect, an awkward question can be raised *about the exercise of this capacity*. Suppose I am conscious of a glass of beer before me: certain properties are then phenomenologically present. Now I reflect on this very fact. The question is: how can the new state of consciousness differ from the original? What becomes phenomenologically present in addition to the properties of the glass of beer? The short answer is 'my consciousness of these things': but what *is* that? I need not become conscious of myself as a human person confronted by a glass of beer. I do not become aware of myself as a brain or immaterial substance so confronted. Yet the new experience – awareness of my awareness of the beer – is not the same as the old one. So unless my-being-conscious-of-a-glass-of-beer has some feature of its own which can be made an object of reflection, even the *capacity* for self-consciousness has not been explained. There would be nothing new for the new act to be conscious of.

Sartre concludes that an act of consciousness must have a primitive way of knowing itself, and that it is this feature which makes it possible for it to serve as intentional object to a further act. But, clearly, this primitive way of knowing itself cannot be accommodated by the doctrine of intentionality, since the whole problem was that acts of consciousness cannot serve as intentional objects unless they have some feature besides that of being directed at an object. Hence Sartre's distinction between thetic and non-thetic consciousness. Thetic consciousness is directedness at intentional objects, be they material things or acts of consciousness: non-thetic consciousness is a non-intentional form of self-awareness which all (human) conscious activity involves, and which makes it possible for us to reflect thetically on our own conscious acts:

> it is the non-reflective consciousness which renders the reflection possible; there is a pre-reflective cogito which is the condition of the Cartesian cogito.
>
> (B&N: xxix; cf. TE: 43ff., PI: 10–11)

And it is non-intentional self-consciousness which supplies the extra component, along with intentionality itself, involved in the being of consciousness. Thus

> the type of existence of consciousness is to be consciousness of itself. And consciousness is aware of itself *in so far as it is consciousness of a transcendent object*. All is therefore clear and lucid in consciousness: the [intentional] object with its characteristic opacity is before consciousness, but consciousness is purely and simply [non-thetic] consciousness of being [thetically] conscious of that object. That is the law of its existence.
>
> (TE: 40)

The *esse* of consciousness does not consist in being perceived, but consists in being non-thetically aware of itself as thetically aware of intentional objects. A mental act, which thereby has an intentional object, is only a *conscious* positing of that intentional object in virtue of its non-thetic self-awareness.

It seems we should agree that the facts of reflection demand that consciousness have some feature beyond directedness-at-an-object. But why should this be a form of self-awareness? Why not some other distinguishing feature? Part of the answer concerns the unity of consciousness mentioned in Chapter 5. Perhaps to say that consciousness has an intimate way of knowing itself is just another way of saying that it exists as a unity or synthesis:

> it is the non-thetic consciousness of counting which is the very condition of my act of adding. If it were otherwise, how would the adding be the unifying theme of my consciousness?
>
> (B&N: xxix)

Furthermore, reflective (thetic) self-consciousness is very reliable: we do not normally find it hard to answer questions about what we are thinking. How could this be unless non-reflective consciousness 'already' knows itself in some way? Attention to the phenomenology helps here too. When you become aware that you have been aware of something for some time, the change is subtle, almost a matter of degree, rather than a drastic phenomenological shift. It is more like turning *up* the lights than turning them *on*. This reinforces the idea that even while you were wholly absorbed in the confronted intentional object, still you were in some way also conscious of being thus conscious. Sartre concludes that

> Consciousness has nothing substantial; it is pure 'appearance' in the sense that it exists only to the degree to which it appears. But it is precisely because consciousness is pure appearance, because it is total emptiness (since the entire world is outside it) – it is because of this identity of appearance and existence within it that it can be considered as the absolute.
>
> (B&N: xxxii; cf. TE: 40–2)

By 'absolute' he means that consciousness, in virtue of its non-thetic awareness, has its own solid mode of being.

This much, though, leaves room for transcendental idealism. Sartre asks

> is consciousness sufficient to provide the foundation for the appearance qua appearance?
>
> (B&N: xxxiii)

His answer is 'no'.

## THE BEING OF APPEARANCE

Sartre builds up to his view by accepting, albeit provisionally, Husserl's claim that appearances constitute reality, so there is no reality 'hidden' by appearances ('appearance' here means 'whatever is given to consciousness', without prior commitment to what this is):

> The appearance does not hide the essence, it reveals it; it *is* the essence ... essence, as the principle of the series [of appearances], is definitely only the concatenation of appearances.
>
> (B&N: xxii)

In the Cartesian scheme, appearances are ideas in the mind, and although the Berkeleyan doctrine that material things are collections of ideas is thus a view which denies that reality is hidden behind appearances, we know that Sartre rejects it. Whatever 'appearances' are according to Sartre, they are not ideas. Indeed, he denies that appearances are things:

> We must renounce those neutral 'givens' which, according to the system of reference chosen, find their place either 'in the world' or 'in the psyche'.
>
> (B&N: xxvii; cf. 625)

So we know that appearance exists outside consciousness, does not have a reality hidden behind it and does not comprise entities called 'appearances'. Among other things, this means that Sartre is committed to the denial of Kantian noumena, as he makes explicit:

> the appearance does not refer to being as Kant's phenomenon refers to the noumenon. Since there is nothing behind the appearance, and since it indicates only itself (and the total series of appearances), it can not be *supported* by any being other than its own.
>
> (B&N: xxiv)

In fact, we have seen that Sartre, as a direct realist in the theory of perception, is committed to the view that consciousness is open to the world of perceptible things – material objects like trees and stones. When he talks of 'appearance', then, he is talking about the perceptible material world. Hence in arguing that the *esse* of appearance does not consist in being perceived, he is arguing against the mind-dependence of material things. That means, in this context, that he is arguing against Husserl's (and anyone else's) transcendental idealism. Since he has already rejected Berkeleyan idealism, that makes him a realist (there is no middle ground).[3] Since he has also rejected Descartes, he is a non-Cartesian realist.

He does concede that appearances are relative to being – '"to appear" supposes in essence somebody to whom to appear' (B&N: xxii). But he seems to treat this as a logical point, on a par with the fact that nothing can be a neighbour unless it is next door to something. He denies that the being of that which appears consists in so appearing, because such an existence would be 'passive', and so would not really be objective. Here he contrasts creating something which is given its own principle of being, from creating 'something' which needs constant upkeep. Only in the first case, he goes on, has some real thing come into existence (B&N: xxxiv–xxxv). So appearance, he urges, must have its own solid mode of being; its being does not consist in being perceived, and even transcendental idealism is unacceptable: 'The phenomenon of In-itself is an abstraction without consciousness but its being is not an abstraction' (B&N: 622).

This may look question-begging. Is not the whole point of idealism, of whatever variety, that the material world does not enjoy a mind-independent existence? But appearance, at least according to the non-Berkeleyan forms of idealism, is supposed to be objective, or at least not 'in' anyone's mind. So ought there not to be something independent, with its own principle of being? And if so, how can it be mind dependent? Thus he goes on that:

> All consciousness is consciousness *of* something. This definition
> . . . can be taken in two very distinct senses: either we under-
> stand by this that consciousness is constitutive of the being of its
> object, or it means that consciousness in its inmost nature is a
> relation to a transcendent being. But the first interpretation . . .
> destroys itself: to be conscious *of* something is to be confronted
> with a concrete and full presence which *is not* consciousness.
>
> (B&N: xxxvi)

He continues:

> consciousness is born *supported by* a being which is not itself.
> This is what we call the ontological proof.
>
> (B&N: xxxvii)

Non-Berkeleyan idealism, at least when coupled with Sartre's claim that consciousness of material things does not involve ideas, does seem dubiously intelligible. If the mind has no resources of its own, how can it 'put' appearances into the objective world?

> consciousness [cannot] 'construct' the transcendent by objectivising elements borrowed from its subjectivity.
>
> (B&N: 171)

How can consciousness become aware of itself as awareness of an intentional object unless the object is already there in its own right? Sartre goes so far as to call his view 'a radical reversal of the idealist position' (B&N: 216), and affirms 'the ontological primacy of the In-itself over the For-itself' (B&N: 619). Rather than the mind constituting the world-as-it-appears, the world somehow constitutes the mind by appearing to it. And the world comes to appear (rather than simply to be) when (non-thetic) awareness of being-appeared-to arises.

The view seems to be this. The material world is 'there anyway'. It cannot appear (be a phenomenon) unless there is something to which it appears (for which it is a phenomenon). But appearances/phenomena are not entities which somehow spring up when a mind arrives. Rather, appearing (be-ing phenomenologically) is a way that material things can be which requires minds (just as I can only be a neighbour if I am next door to someone). But material things appear just as they are anyway (appearance hides nothing). Thus, material things exist either alone in-themselves or as appearances for consciousness:

> it is through the For-itself that the meaning of being appears. This totalization of being *adds nothing* to being; it is nothing but the manner in which being is revealed as not being the For-itself, the manner in which *there is* being . . . But the fact of revealing being as a totality does not touch being any more than the fact of counting two cups on the table touches the existence or nature of either of them.
>
> (B&N: 181)

This is Sartrean, non-Cartesian, realism. Recall that Cartesian realism entails the two doctrines

1 The world could exist without any minds in it.
2 Minds could exist without any surrounding material world or environment.

Whereas Berkeleyan idealism in effect drops (1) and retains (2),

Sartre's 'radical reversal of idealism' involves dropping (2) and retaining (1).

## EXTERNALISM: THE MIND AIN'T IN THE HEAD

It is illuminating here to reflect briefly on what has come to be called *externalism* in the philosophy of mind. This is the view that the mind ain't in the head, or (more lucidly) that at least some aspects of the mind entail appropriate embedding in the world.[4] One much-discussed example is the view that you cannot suppose that water is wet, or have any other mental states with water as intentional object, unless you are appropriately related to samples of the liquid. On this view, creatures on waterless worlds could no more think about water than they could swim in it. Aspects of mind such as *thinking about water* do not simply involve matters in the brain or body, but embrace the appropriate parts of the world.

Now I have had the right sort of intercourse with water, so I can think about it. But neither an envatted replica of my brain, nor an immaterial mind in a world otherwise empty save for an evil deceiver, has had the appropriate intercourse. So neither brain nor immaterial mind could have water-thoughts, according to our externalist. This appears to entail, contrary to what, for example, the materialistic Cartesian realist claims, that the envatted brain does not embody a subject psychologically the same as me, despite being an atom-for-atom replica of my brain now. I can have water-thoughts, whereas the subject (if any) embodied in the envatted brain cannot, so *there* is a psychological difference. Externalists are thus more or less hostile to one strand of Cartesian realism: they deny the material-world-independence of the mind. Nevertheless, this leaves open the status of the material world. In particular, externalists need not deny the mind-independence of the material world, and so they can consistently hold that the material world could exist even if there were not and never had been any minds. According to externalists as they usually present themselves, the dependency all runs in one direction: mind depends upon material world, but not vice versa.

The parallels with Sartre's 'radical reversal of idealism' are obvious and striking. Indeed, given his emphasis on intentionality, his rejection of ideas and his activity-based model of conscious mental life, it is hard to see how he can *fail* to be committed to some form of externalism (although, of course, he did not consider this question explicitly). Thus:

> The For-itself is outside itself in the In-itself since it causes itself to be defined by what it is not; the first bond between the In-itself and the For-itself is therefore a bond of being.
>
> (B&N: 177)

## EXTERNALIST PHENOMENOLOGY

Now that we have established what Sartre's view is, however, we need to turn back to unfinished business. This is the problem of accounting for the apparent presence of perceptible properties in the absence of anything to have them. When I see that a brown blackbird is nearby, the property of *being brown* figures in the experience in a way that it does not when I merely think the same thing. One might try to explain this in terms of the fact that in seeing but not merely thinking, the properties of the seen thing act on the sense organs. Unfortunately, as we have noted, properties can be phenomenologically present when nothing of the right sort acts on the sense organs. I may image a blackbird, or misperceive and see something as elliptical when it is round, or have a hallucination of pink elephants. Indirect realism, as we remarked, is standardly defended on the basis of these points by way of the Argument from Illusion. Indirect realism has been refuted, but Sartre's direct realism still faces the problem.

So how does he proceed? How does he cope with misrepresentation and hallucination? The short and extraordinary answer is that he does not. Despite the absolute centrality of this issue to the truth or even coherence of his view, Sartre says next to nothing about it. In what follows, then, we depart for a short time from anything he explicitly considered, although we are still concerned with the implications of his stated views, and we shall work back to suggestive hints in what he does say.

How can Sartre manage without representations? The only hope seems to be to take a hint from his apparent proposal about imaging, and reapply it to perception. The idea in the imaging case, recall, was to construe the phenomenology of imaging as parasitic on that of perception: one images by exploiting the capacity to perceive (Chapter 5). The analogous proposal now would be to think of hallucination and misperception as parasitic on veridical perception. On this view, the metaphysically prior notion is that of veridical perception: this is what needs to be accounted for first if matters phenomenological are to be understood. We need to say first what it is like to see the world aright, and then turn to account for seeing it awrong.

As before, this has to be distinct from the merely psychological proposal that no one can hallucinate or misperceive until the systems needed for veridical perception are up and running. Even an indirect realist can agree with that: for it is quite consistent with the proposal to insist that the systems needed for veridical perception include scanners, inner pictures and the like. The direct realist's claim has to be the metaphysical one that hallucination and misperception *by their very nature* are to be understood in terms of veridical perception, which itself in turn must be accounted for without appeal to inner pictures or any of the other accoutrements of indirect realism. O'Beth sees a dagger, Macbeth hallucinates one, but they are enjoying experiences indistinguishable from the first-person point of view. The explanatory programme adopted by indirect realists starts off with something like Macbeth's hallucinatory state as basic, and explains O'Beth's perceptual state in terms of it plus a relation to a real dagger. The direct realist must proceed in the other direction, and take O'Beth's state as the place to start. Somehow, Macbeth's state is to be fundamentally conceived as a redundant or limiting case of O'Beth's: O'Beth's state is not to be conceived as a result of an augmentation of an explanatorily more fundamental inner state which he shares with Macbeth.[5]

The minimum requirement for this externalist programme to work is that the doctrine be taken seriously, and not just treated as a reflection of the fact that we *describe* mental states in environmental terms.[6] This probably requires that we think of environment-involving descriptions of experiences as characterising them in 'inside-looking-out' terms, that is by describing them as ways-of-being-open-to-the-world. I literally describe how you experience the world by describing THE WORLD as it appears to you. This approach requires in turn that we think of the description of experience as involving a sort of imaginative projection into your point of view, a recentring which enables us to envisage how the world strikes you and thus describe what it is like to have your experience:

the Other's body is perceived wholly differently than other bodies: for in order to perceive it we always move to it from what is outside of it, in space and time; we apprehend its gesture 'against the current' by a sort of inversion of time and space. To perceive the Other is to make known to oneself what he is by means of the world.

(B&N: 346; cf. 254)

Characterising a person's phenomenology, on this externalist conception, is not a matter of saying what it is like in the recesses of their skull (the 'outside-looking-in' conception), but a way of conveying their experiential point of view on their surroundings. It involves a kind of make-believe, in which we put ourselves into the other's shoes and say how things seem from there. And the crucial point is that the THINGS concerned are the objects with which the subject is confronted.[7]

If this sort of approach to experience and how it is to be conceived is adopted, then misperception and hallucination could come out as parasitic on veridical perception as follows. In coming to appreciate a deluded or hallucinatory experience, one still needs to go in for the kind of imaginative projection required in the case of veridical perception. So first, we need to see you as a point of view on your surroundings, and as such deploy whatever resources this requires. Then we have to come to a conception of those surroundings which squares with your sincere but manifestly out-of-kilter descriptions of what you confront. This requires further imagination, as well as the associated (and equally parasitic) capacity to visualise. We grasp your hallucinatory state when we picture the scene as it appears to you. What is going on when he hallucinates a pink elephant? Things appear to him like *this* [use your imagination!].

This is most likely to seem unsatisfactory on the grounds that it gives no model of *what is going on* when someone hallucinates: no model in terms of underlying processes or whatever. Instead, the focus is on what *we* do in envisaging how it is for *you*. Correct, but this is no objection. Here I think we do come close to some of Sartre's stated views. Certainly the general approach chimes in well with his activity-based model of conscious mental life, and with his idea that in unreflective experience I am 'plunged into the world of objects . . . [which] constitute the unity of my consciousnesses' (TE: 49). The externalistic flavour of this second claim hardly needs pointing out, while one ought not to be surprised, if conscious mental life is an activity, that conveying its precise character should require imagination, recentring and other forms of imitative endeavour:

> To listen to conversation is to 'speak with', not simply because we imitate in order to interpret, but because we originally project ourselves towards the possibles and because we must understand *in terms of the world*.
>
> (B&N: 515)

At a more general level, this construal of externalism echoes Sartre's idea that understanding thinking beings and their works involves a different kind of knowledge from that gained by naturalistic or scientific approaches. To our heart's content we can see people as complex animals, physical systems with this or that physical inheritance, overlain and modified by informational input, and issuing in outputs of various bodily sorts. But if we want to know what it is like to be them – if we want to understand their experience of the world as they do, or *see them as subjects* – then we need to take a different approach, and go in for the sort of imaginative projection mentioned above.[8] In so doing we come to understand them in a new way, a way which is not guaranteed to be available to one who sees them simply as complex natural systems:

> The environment can act on the subject only to the exact extent that he comprehends it; that is, transforms it into a situation. Hence no objective description of this environment could be of any use to us.
>
> (B&N: 572)

One wants to press the above objection by asking how the alleged special process of understanding comes about. Presumably if I imaginatively project and thus gain access to a special kind of understanding of you, then this can only be due to the functioning of *my* brain and body, so surely some account of the understanding can be given in 'objective' terms after all? No. Once again, we either see me-the-understander as a mere physical system, in which case we have no guaranteed access to what it is like to-be-me-understanding, or we take a different view of me and understand me as understanding you. The point is that there is no reduction of the one kind of knowledge to the other: interpretation

goes all the way down. It is not that the sciences of the body have
no story to tell, simply that it can never be the whole story. This
is the profound claim shared by existentialism and other forms
of real externalism: that to be minded is to be embedded in a
world or 'situation', and that there is an aspect of the manner
of embeddedness which is in a sense 'magical' (B&N: 295), or
(more soberly) inaccessible from an objective point of view:

> The body is . . . *the only psychic object*. But if we consider that the
> body is a transcended transcendence, then the perception of it
> can not *by nature* be of the same type as that of inanimate objects.
> We must not understand by this that the perception is pro-
> gressively enriched but that originally it is of another structure.
>
> (B&N: 347)

This aspect of Sartre's account of experience will be considered
further in the following chapter, where his views on the traditional problem of other minds are discussed.

## ELEMENTS OF IDEALISM?

Although Sartre is a form of realist, there are places where he
sounds like a transcendental idealist. To get a fully rounded
picture of his position, we need to see why.

It is partly because, as we have seen, there are *some* aspects of the
perceived world which he does believe to be mind-dependent.
Things strike us as difficult, or desirable, or hateful, or good or
bad. We perceive nothingnesses. Sartre holds that in experiencing
things thus we experience them as objectively thus: values and the
rest strike us as belonging to the world. But he also holds that
nothing has value or significance in itself: things are only valuable
or significant because we value them, and parallel remarks apply
to nothingnesses. All of this, if you like, is transcendental idealism
with respect to these things: they are not felt 'in the breast' (that
would be, as it were, Berkeleyan idealism with respect to them),
but they are nevertheless 'put there' or projected on to the material
world by us. But the world is there first to be projected on to (recall
the 'ontological proof').

Relatedly, Sartre focuses on aspects of social being: we see
things as amenities, and thus as things which can only be understood in the context of broader social concerns (B&N: 423ff.). A
boat for hire, unlike a piece of driftwood, is not seen by me just as

a convenient way of getting *me* downstream (cf. B&N: 510–11). This sort of perceived significance or instrumentality certainly is mind- or agent-dependent, yet this does not prevent the amenities from being perfectly objective material things. The boat is no less real than the piece of driftwood:

> The thing, in so far as it both rests in the quiet beatitude of indifference and yet points beyond it to tasks to be performed which make known to it what it has to be, is an instrument or utensil.
>
> (B&N: 200)

Instruments are material objects which are normally literally constituted by us, and apart from thoughts about what is theoretically or logically possible, they would not have existed if minds had not. But this is not transcendental idealism about instruments themselves, although it might encourage careless talk in that direction. For in so far as the world is viewed as a world of signs and instruments, it 'remains strictly human' (B&N: 218). More, given the extent to which I experience the world in terms of my own plans, expectations, etc.,

> the totality of instruments is the exact correlate of my possibilities; and as I *am* my possibilities, the order of instruments in the world is the image of my possibilities projected in the in-itself; i.e. the image of what I am.
>
> (B&N: 200)

The world is 'my world', friendly (or at least familiar), shaped by my concerns. Although 'being is everywhere, opposite me, around me', still if

> I want to grasp this being ... I no longer find anything but *myself*.
>
> (B&N: 218)

All of this is good phenomenology – but it is clearly not idealistic. Here is a harder example:

> A being is fragile if it carries in its being a definite possibility of non-being. But ... it is through man that fragility comes into being ... the relation of individualizing limitation which man enters into with one being ... causes fragility to enter this being as the appearance of a permanent possibility of non-being ...

Thus it is man who renders cities destructible, precisely because he posits them as fragile and as precious and because he adopts a system of protective measures with regard to them. It is because of this ensemble of measures that an earthquake or a volcanic eruption can *destroy* these cities or these human constructions . . . It is necessary then to realise that destruction is an essentially human thing and that *it is man* who destroys his cities through the agency of earthquakes or directly, who destroys his ships through the agency of cyclones or directly . . . In addition, destruction although coming into being through man, is *an objective fact* and not a thought.

(B&N: 8–9)

Leave aside the thought that both ship and city are artefacts, and so would not have existed without minds. Icicles and butterflies are fragile, and earthquakes destroy forests as well as cities. In any case, the fact that something needs minds to come into existence does not entail that it needs minds to go out of existence or to be fragile. A vase could survive a holocaust which wiped out all sentient life but remain fragile, and shatter on toppling in the wind.

Even here, though, Sartre distinguishes destruction from the mere rearrangement of masses (B&N: 8), and claims that although the latter can occur without our input, the former cannot: and for this reason alone the passage is not idealistic. Part of his point is that fragility involves a 'definite possibility of non-being': seeing something as fragile is seeing its possibilities for breakage. And such possibilities, for Sartre, come into the world because of us. But he may also have it in mind that fragility involves a reference to a human-sized perspective. Forces of all types cause the disintegration of all sorts of material things. But to be fragile a thing must break *easily*, where this means 'on the application of forces which are quite small in normal human contexts'. If we were denser or more boisterous, then wooden chairs would be fragile (would be easily breakable in ordinary human contexts). As it is, we exclude them from the class of fragile things, but only because of how we are. They could remain the same in themselves but still be fragile in different circumstances. The point is not that 'fragile' is vague, but that the division between fragile and non-fragile things, all vagueness aside, is an arbitrary line drawn through the world from the perspective of human-sized concerns. Like colour, fragility is 'relative' (to us).

A further point is that 'fragile' is evaluative, due to its link with 'break'. Things undergo all sorts of change, but only some count as breakage. Partly this is because we have certain uses to which we want to put things, and so see some changes as involving breakage rather than more or less extreme modification. A scratched car is not broken, whereas a squashed car is, simply because the second but not the first change subverts the car's normal function. Some of this carries over to Sartre's claim about the destruction of cities. A city is changing all the time, but only some of this – to do with its fitness for people to live in – counts as destruction. One thinks here of shifting sands, arranged and rearranged by wind and tide. Nothing is either made or destroyed, all is flux. Then humans arrive, and either shore up banks of the stuff against the sea, or shelter behind the dunes. Now the possibility of destruction has arrived too: from now on, one change is not as good as another. This bank is now destructible because I live behind it . . .

You can see what he's getting at, but it does not do to be too impressed. Whether or not a tree is destroyed or a rock shattered out of existence or a molecule decomposed may be vague matters, but they are nothing to do with human interests. Trees, rocks and molecules, independently of any interest of ours or function we may give them, have their own (perhaps vague) principles of being, in accordance with which they come into and go out of existence. Whether or not these matters are *significant* (to us) does depend on our interests. But whether or not they occur does not. It is worth quoting here the famous passage in *Nausea*[9] where Roquentin confronts the being of the tree-root:

> The roots of the chestnut tree sank into the ground beneath my bench. I couldn't remember it was a root any more. Words had vanished, and with them *the meanings of things, the way things are to be used, the feeble points of reference which men have traced on their surface.* (emphases added)

Stripped of all the meaning it has for humans, the root still has its own grotesque being.

So far, then, we have managed to explain away idealist passages in Sartre. But there are yet more difficult ones. On space and time, he seems unequivocal:

> The spatializing being is the For-itself as co-present to the whole and to the 'this'.

(B&N: 184)

Universal time comes into the world through the For-itself. The In-itself is not adapted to temporality.

(B&N: 204)

So with motion too (since this is change of place over time):

a For-itself is necessary in order for motion to exist.

(B&N: 209)

Also, there are places where Sartre seems committed to the view that the non-conscious world is, in itself, a 'fullness' or 'plenitude', an undifferentiated mass of porridge-like stuff which is moulded into the known world by us:[10]

The In-itself is not diversity; it is not multiplicity; and in order for it to receive multiplicity as the characteristic of its being-in-the-midst-of-the-world, a being must arise which is simultaneously present to each In-itself isolated in its own identity. It is through human reality that multiplicity comes into the world.

(B&N: 137)

There is enough of the noumenal about this 'full plenitude' to give pause. Still, if these claims could be construed as phenomenological, to do with how the world appears rather than how it is in itself, there would be no problem. So it is to be noted well that in very many passages concerning the 'undifferentiated' nature of Being In-itself, Sartre is unproblematically on the phenomenological plane. Thus the café in which one expected to meet the absent Pierre

is a fullness of being . . . I enter this cafe to search for Pierre . . . each element of the setting, a person, a table, a chair, attempts to isolate itself, to lift itself upon the ground constituted by the totality of the other objects, only to fall back once more into the undifferentiation of this ground; it melts into the ground.

(B&N: 9–10)

This is not the claim that the café dissolves into porridge under my searching glance! Similar remarks apply to Sartre's discussion of perceptual salience:

The 'this' is the being which I at present am not, in so far as it appears on the ground of the totality of being . . . it is what is revealed on the undifferentiated ground of being . . . Yet it can always dissolve again into this undifferentiated totality when another 'this' arises.

(B&N: 182)

Indeed, Sartre is explicit that 'dissolving' and 'undifferentiation' should not be taken literally:

the 'this' is revealed as 'this' by 'a withdrawal into the ground of the world' on the part of all the other 'thises'; its determination, which is the origin of all determinations, is a negation. [But] we must understand that this negation – seen from the point of view of the 'this' – is wholly ideal [i.e. doesn't really occur in the realm of the In-itself]. It adds nothing to being and subtracts nothing from it. The being confronted as 'this' is what it is and does not cease being it; it does not become.

(B&N: 183)

If we suppose that the For-itself is present to one *this*, the other thises exist at the same time 'in the world' but by virtue of being undifferentiated; they constitute the ground on which the *this* confronted is raised in relief.

(B&N: 189)

Fine. But what of the cases of space and time? Even here, the awkward passages cited above have to be squared with

The existence of space is the proof that the For-itself by causing being 'to be there' [i.e. phenomenologically present] adds nothing to being. Space is the ideality of the synthesis.

(B&N: 184)

and

The inkwell at the moment I perceive it *already* exists in the three temporal dimensions [viz. past, present, future].

(B&N: 204; emphasis added)

Sartre's discussion of these matters is among the more opaque parts of B&N, and I am far from clear about what he means. But he seems explicitly to reject a Kantian approach to space:

it would be useless to conceive of space as a form imposed on phenomena by the *a priori* structure of our sensibility.

(B&N: 184)

and it is at least possible that he is embracing the idea that space is not in itself a real thing, but consists simply in the fact that material things have spatial relations with one another. On such a view there is no such thing as 'absolute' position in space, but simply position relative to this or that chosen thing. This may be the import of

> Space can not be a being. It is a moving relation between beings which are unrelated ... [it] is pure exteriority ... When the exteriority of indifference is hypostatized as a substance existing in and through itself ... it is made the object of a type of study under the title of geometry.
>
> (B&N: 184–5)

As regards time, Sartre may be registering that the idea of change makes reference to a time-bound point of view, since otherwise one slips into thinking of material things as laid out in a static, unchanging framework:

> Temporality in so far as it is grasped objectively is thus a pure phantom, for it does not give itself as the temporality of the For-itself nor as the temporality which the In-itself has to be ... Consequently, the unchangeable *this* is revealed across a flicker-ing and an infinite parcelling out of phantom In-itselfs. This is how that glass or that table is revealed to me. They do not endure; they are. Time flows over them.
>
> (B&N: 205)

It would be rash to claim that the foregoing explains away all traces of transcendental idealism in Sartre. The thought remains that he may have been so imbued with the idealism of those who influenced him – Kant, Hegel, Husserl – that he sometimes lapses into talk which is incompatible with his official view. But this gives little cause to claim that Sartre is 'really' an idealist. Nor need we regard his position as hopelessly flawed, since such idealistic intrusions as there are seem to have no ineliminable structural place in the system. One the contrary: Sartre can be emphatic and unambiguous when it comes to points of deep doctrine and statements of intention. And in such places he is a realist, as we have seen.

## NOTES AND FURTHER READING

1   J.-P. Sartre, *Words* tr. I. Clephane (Harmondsworth: Penguin, 1967): 34.
2   Here we collide with another problem. As noted in the previous

chapter, it is not true that all of the information coming in through my senses is thereby available to my consciousness, even if it has an effect on my reactions to the stimulations. Some information guides me without making any sort of phenomenological impact. So perhaps the sexy lips fall into the category of incoming information which is not available to consciousness in any way. Perhaps this suggests an acceptable sense in which non-human animals are not really conscious of, but only responsive to information from, their surroundings. But the matter here is extremely delicate. After all, we can learn to notice people's lips and pupils, and to be conscious that this is what we are doing, quite easily. So perhaps they fall into a sort of phenomenological no man's land in the present example, hovering somehow on the brink of consciousness, but not quite available to self-consciousness without more ado. Recall here Sartre's point that some facts about consciousness can only be uncovered after prolonged Phenomenological analysis.

3   This is not to say that there is only one form of realism: as remarked, Sartre is not a *Cartesian realist*. It seems that he is thus also committed to denying what is sometimes called *metaphysical realism* (see H. Putnam, *Realism and Reason* (Cambridge: Cambridge University Press, 1983)) and sometimes *Platonism* (see M. Morris, *The Good and the True* (Oxford: Clarendon Press, 1992)). If so, then he is probably committed to denying the correspondence theory of truth, as Putnam argues. But this is not so much because there is something wrong with the notion of truth or 'objective reality', but because there is nothing mental (ideas or whatever) to correspond to it. Putnam often comes perilously close to missing this point (e.g. *Realism*: 144–7, 207), and it is not clear that Morris' formulations of 'conceptualism' can be sustained if the point is given due weight – Morris, *The Good*: 15–20.

4   Externalism is so called because it involves the claim that aspects of mind are dependent on matters external to the individual who enjoys them. But this is in fact a misleading terminology, given the traditional conception of the 'external world' as comprising whatever is outside the mind. For externalism is precisely the view that matters external to the individual (i.e. beyond his or her skin) are not external to the individual's *mind*. Issues are further clouded by the fact that 'external' in 'external world' is often given an epistemological sense so that, for example, even if the brain *is* the mind, still it belongs to the 'external world'. Whereas, of course, the sense of 'external' involved in externalism is ontological. In so far as externalism is the denial of the claim that the mind is (literally) in the head, there are at least three forms of it. One is embodied in the Wittgensteinian (and existentialist) claim, for example, that understanding is constituted by certain habits and practices rather than by alleged underlying processes or structures. On this approach, 'the human body is the best picture of the human soul': L. Wittgenstein, *Philosophical Investigations* tr. G.E.M. Anscombe (Oxford: Blackwell, 1953) §IIiv. Another version, as introduced in the text, stresses that the aspects of mind in question require the subject to be embedded appropriately in the right sort of physical

environment. For this sort of view see H. Putnam, 'The meaning of "meaning"' in his *Mind, Language and Reality* (Cambridge: Cambridge University Press, 1975). Yet another form of externalism stresses that certain aspects of mind can only be enjoyed if the subject is part of the right sort of society or community. For this externalism, see T. Burge, 'Individualism and the mental', *Midwest Studies in Philosophy* vol. IV (1979) (on some interpretations, of course, Wittgenstein held a similar view). The three forms are plainly distinct. The first, but not the second or third, is as it stands compatible with the idea that the entire universe should consist simply of one thinking thing (a body-in-a-vat). The second, but not the third, is at least compatible with the thought that only one thinker should ever have existed. And the third, but not the second or first, may even be compatible with the basic idea of Berkeley's idealism (a community of 'external world'-independent minds). Of course, the three claims can be combined (or confused). One chief source of confusion is the absurd tendency to use 'in the head' metaphorically as a synonym for 'solipsistic'. This disguises the existence and importance of the first kind of externalism. For possible elements of the third sort of externalism in Sartre, see the discussion of shame in Chapter 8 below. For general discussions of externalism, see for example P. Pettit and J. McDowell eds, *Subject, Thought, and Context* (Oxford: Oxford University Press, 1986) and G. McCulloch, *The Game of the Name* (Oxford: Oxford University Press, 1989) ch. 6.

5   It is tacit in the text that direct realism in perception is a form of externalism as previously introduced. But Jonathan Dancy distinguishes between the object of a normal act of perception, and 'the perceptual state as an object-less residue' which may be shared by the perceiver and an appropriate hallucinator, his guiding thought being that 'most direct realists are internalists in this respect' (J. Dancy, *Introduction to Contemporary Epistemology* (Oxford: Blackwell, 1985): 170). But it is exceedingly difficult to see any difference between this position and a modified form of indirect realism: see G. McCulloch, 'The very idea of the phenomenological', *Proceedings of the Aristotelian Society*, vol. XCIII, 1993.

6   It is possible, indeed orthodox, to pay lip-service to externalism whilst remaining a closet internalist. Certainly, it can be agreed, it is impossible to *suppose that water is wet* unless one is appropriately linked to samples of water. But, the thought continues, this does not rule out the possibility that the relevant envatted brain embodies a subject which is psychologically the same as me. For it leaves open the idea that the envatted brain's states have the same *intrinsic* (or 'narrow') properties as do my brain's states, and that it is these intrinsic properties which determine psychological identity: see J. Fodor, *Psychosemantics* (Cambridge, Mass.: MIT Press, 1987) ch. 2. This position is clearly internalistic in spirit – a Cartesian realist could accept it – although, given its small concession to the externalist over how mental states are described or identified, one might at a stretch think of it as a watered-down version of externalism. The position in C. McGinn, *Mental Content* (Oxford: Blackwell, 1989), although

*described* as real externalism, seems to differ only in name from this watered-down variety. The proposal in the text is a more radical version, and it is hard to see how Sartre could countenance anything less, given his rejection of mental representations.

7  For an excellent account of this sort of enterprise see Jane Heal, 'Replication and functionalism' in *Language, Mind and Logic* ed. J. Butterfield (Cambridge: Cambridge University Press, 1986). Compare W.V. Quine, *Word and Object* (Cambridge, Mass.: MIT Press, 1960): 218–19.

8  This point is conceded, in effect, in Quine *Word*:

> In the strictest scientific spirit we can report all the behaviour, verbal and otherwise, that may underlie our imputations of propositional attitudes, and we may go on to speculate as we please upon the causes and effects of this behaviour; but so long as we do not switch muses, the essentially dramatic idiom of propositional attitudes will find no place.
>
> (219)

Quine concludes from this that in understanding others as subjects we are not 'limning the true and ultimate structure of reality' (221), i.e. are not describing facts about the world. But a more balanced response is simply to accept that there is more to know about the contents of the world than can be gleaned in 'the strictest scientific spirit'.

9  J.-P. Sartre, *Nausea* tr. Robert Baldick (Harmondsworth: Penguin, 1965).

10  This is quite a common interpretation of Sartre: see for example T.L.S. Sprigge, *Theories of Existence* (Harmondsworth: Penguin, 1985) ch. 7, and M. Hammond, J. Howarth and R. Keat, *Understanding Phenomenology* (Oxford: Blackwell, 1992) ch. 4. The idea that we somehow fashion the familiar world out of a formless In-itself also sometimes seems to creep into the work of those who oppose metaphysical realism (see note 3), as though the unavailability of truth-by-correspondence threatens all forms of realism: see for example David Wiggins, 'On singling out an object determinately' in *Subject*, P. Pettit and J. McDowell eds: 'It is we . . . who impose lines on nature' (170). It is worth repeating that the problems of metaphysical realism seem to be more to do with its non-externalistic, non-existentialist idea that the mind can be set over against the world and questions about correspondence raised. Realism requires an overhaul of the theory of mind, not the theory of reality:

> When this kind of [metaphysical] realism is rejected, the result is not that we are left wildly improvising. A contribution to stability is still made by the natures of the things to which we apply our words. It is just that another contribution is made by the ways in which we find it natural to apply them, and the two contributions cannot be disentangled from one another. (D. Pears, *The False Prison* vol. 1 (Oxford: Oxford University Press, 1987): 31–2.)

Correspondence requires that the two contributions be disentangled.

# Chapter 8

# Shame

A man evaporates without an eye-witness.

Sartre[1]

We come now to what Sartre calls a new kind of 'ontological structure' of our being, a

> relation to myself as subject [which nevertheless] reveals to me
> a being which is *my* being without being-for-me.
>
> (B&N: 221)

His example is shame. This is a form of consciousness, and hence involves non-thetic self-awareness: 'as such, . . . it is accessible to reflection'. Moreover, it is intentional, or directed at an object – me. But although it is reflexive it is not, says Sartre, primarily a phenomenon of reflection. Rather,

> it is in its primary structure shame *before somebody* . . . the Other
> is the indispensable mediator between myself and me. I am
> ashamed of myself *as I appear* to the Other.
>
> (B&N: 221–2)

What does this mean?

## THE PROBLEMS OF THE OTHER

Sartre's views on shame are best seen initially in the context of the traditional Problem of Other Minds. Roughly, the problem is this. I have a direct acquaintance with my own thoughts, feelings, sensory experience and so on. I live among other humans who are like me in very many respects, and I take it that these other humans have a mental life too. But I have no direct acquaintance with this supposed mental life of others: I don't literally think their thoughts and feel their pains. Rather, I just assume that it exists on the basis of their behaviour: they wince and exclaim when I stick pins in them, purr when I stroke them (sometimes), and so on. Worse, the idea of having such an acquaintance appears to make no sense. Suppose you say you have toothache, and a clever scientist connects our brains with a cable and tells us that I will now be able to feel your ache. Well, if I am to know it as an ache – have the usual acquaintance with it that I have with other aches – I will have to feel it as I feel my own toothaches. But now surely this is *my* ache that I am feeling, and the questions whether it is also felt by you, or at least 'matches' yours, or indeed whether you have one at all, are unapproached. (The same goes, of course, if someone claims to have telepathic access to another's aches.) All in all, then, why do I so confidently proceed as if other humans have a mental life when I not only do not, but could not, have any direct acquaintance with it?

The answer may seem easy. People very often tell me that they have toothache, that they think that grass is green and so on. And even if they are always lying, they must have a mental life in order to lie! This begs the question. All that I am entitled to is that others *utter words* such as 'I have toothache' and 'I think that grass is green'. And it does not follow that they understand these words, or mean them in the way that I mean mine. To assume they do is to assume that they have a mental life, and this is the question at issue. After all, parrots and tape recorders produce English sentences which I can understand, but this hardly shows that they have a mental life, or know what they are 'saying'.

The problem is more profound than it may seem at first. To see this, compare it to the Other Brains Problem. Harry has a transparent skull, and everyone can see his brain pulsing away in there. No one's head has ever been opened, and no one else has a transparent skull. Harry (or anyone else capable of thought) can wonder whether he is special in having a brain inside his head, and even if he assumes that others do because of their other similarities to him, we can wonder whether this assumption is reasonable. But this is an empirical challenge, on a par with 'I wonder if all apples have pips in them, like this one?' We can not only make sense of the idea that other heads (or apples) may be opened up and inspected, but only have to wait for the de-velopment of appropriate technology in order to get started. In the other minds case, by contrast, we have seen that technology does not seem to the point (cf. B&N: 251), and that the whole idea of inspecting another's mind seems senseless.

The problem is similar to other traditional sceptical issues: (1) I have direct acquaintance with my experiences, but assume that they concern an objective world. Why make this further assumption? (2) I have direct acquaintance with the present, and assume that some presently available things (e.g. my memories) are evidence that there were past times before now. But might not the world have sprung into being five seconds ago, complete with bogus fossil 'records', bogus 'memories' and so on? (3) We have examined a good sample of emeralds and they are all green. We take this as good evidence that all other, unexamined emeralds are green. But why assume that the unexamined resembles the examined? (4) I can observe the track in the chamber, and I assume that it is the effect of an unobservable subatomic particle. But why?

The sceptical syndrome consists of a domain of apparently known evidential truths, a further domain of claims made on this evidential basis, and an awkward question: why assume so confidently that the evidence supports the further claims?[2] In the other minds case, the evidential domain comprises the behaviour of others, and the further claims concern their supposed mental life. However, there are various disanalogies between the cases, and in particular the other minds problem seems especially virulent. As far as claims about the unexamined emeralds are concerned, I can at least go looking to check. And although I may not similarly be able to go back to check that the past is 'there' (in a sense this would be checking out my future anyway), I can at least make sense of the thought that there are times before this one of which I might have had direct acquaintance. Similarly, I can at least imagine that I might have been smaller, and able to perceive subatomic particles directly. And once we have left behind the Cartesian realist idea that we cannot be acquainted with material things, but only with ideas of them, the thought is available that this experienced tree is there whether I experience it or not: it transcends my experience of it, and is there to be experienced again. So in all these cases we can make good sense of what it is for our sceptically challenged claims to be *true*, even if we cannot meet the challenge. But in the other minds case, as mentioned, we can make no parallel sense of checking our claims about others directly, and so it is arguable that when I, for instance, attribute thoughts and feelings to another human, I do not even really *know what I am saying*, because I do not have any notion of what sort of fact I am trying to describe. The operative principle here is that *one only has a conception of a kind of fact if one knows what it would be to confront an example*. But I could not confront your experiences in the appropriate way. Thus, what starts out as run-of-the-mill scepticism about other minds rapidly seems to turn into *solipsism*, the view that all experience and thought is *mine*.[3]

## THE 'REEF OF SOLIPSISM'

Sartre describes graphically how such a situation gets under way almost immediately for Descartes:

> The Other's soul is . . . separated from mine by all the distance which separates first my soul from my body, then my body from the Other's body, and finally the Other's body from his soul.
>
> (B&N: 223)

At most, he goes on, only the Other's body (behaviour) can be present to me: the soul is, at best, posited. But in fact the situation is worse than this. First, according to Descartes, not even the Other's body is present to me, just my ideas of it (and the same goes for *my* body, of course). This may seem to offer us hope: why cannot I similarly, then, have an idea of the Other's soul? This would at least show that solipsism is not inevitable, although traditional Cartesian scepticism about the 'external world' (including our bodies) remains, and even if that were solved, the sceptical problem of other minds would persist: why could there not be human bodies which did not contain an immaterial ego, but functioned like automata? Thus

> If animals are machines, why shouldn't the man whom I see pass in the street be one?
>
> (B&N: 224)

However, the supposition that one could have an idea of another's soul or mind is problematic. This is obvious if an idea is thought of as a mental picture – what would a picture of a mind be like? – and scarcely less so if we do not enquire into what ideas could otherwise be. For whatever they could be, to have an idea of another's mind would be to know what sort of fact is involved in their having one (just as to have an idea of a cat is to know what it would be for there to be a cat). And this, we have seen, is what we apparently cannot do: '[Cartesian] realism provides no place for the intuition of the Other' (B&N: 223).[4] Descartes' position seems to lead first to scepticism and then to solipsism by its very nature. Of course, we rejected Descartes' position anyway in Chapter 6, but neither the Problem of Other Minds, as set up at the beginning of the present chapter, nor the threat of solipsism, seems to *require* a Cartesian starting-point (though see below for more on this).

## APPROACHING THE SCEPTICISM

Even if we forget Descartes, leave aside the apparent alarming fall into solipsism and just concentrate on the sceptical question, it is hard to make progress. So, assuming for the moment that I know *what it is* for there to be other minds, how can I know *that there are* any? One suggestion is the Argument from Analogy: in my own case, I see the pin enter the skin, feel the pain, am aware of exclaiming and jerking away. In your case, I see two out of three (the pin going in, your overt reaction): is it not reasonable to assume, on the basis of your other similarities to me, that you have the intervening pain also? In fact it is not particularly reasonable – scarcely more so than arguing that you probably have a mole under your left arm because I do[5] – and in any case, complains Sartre, this argument would at best give only 'conjectural' knowledge (B&N: 224). Yet surely I am *certain* that you have a mind? Another suggestion is the behaviouristic one that all there is to having a mind is being capable of the right sort of behaviour. On this approach, since I know what your behavioural capabilities are, I know you have a mind. As we already know, Sartre rejects behaviourism since it squeezes consciousness out of the mental picture altogether (STE: 37–41; see Chapter 2 above). And he is of course right: we all know that there is more to feeling a pain, say, than saying 'ouch' and jerking away. There is also consciousness of the sensation, and this is something that behaviourism misses out:

> A psychology which wants to be exact and objective, like the 'behaviourism' of Watson, is really only solipsism as a working hypothesis. It will not try to deny within the field of my experience the presence of objects which we shall call 'psychic

beings' but will merely practise a sort of *epoché* with respect to the existence of systems of representations organized by a subject and located outside my experience.

(B&N: 229)

So neither analogy nor behaviourism is any use. A better idea is to think of another's mind as a sort of explanatory posit.[6] On this more or less orthodox contemporary view, the claim that humans have minds is on a par with the claim that things have internal structures which are causally responsible for their overt performance. The mind would be like a clock's mechanism, or the liver, or the brain. Indeed, given the problems with Descartes' immaterialism (Chapter 6), and what we know about the brain's role in producing behaviour, why not simply say that the mind *is* the brain, at least where humans are concerned (it might be some other organ in other conceivable creatures)? Then the sceptical problem of other minds after all reduces to the sceptical problem of other brains, which as we saw above is not particularly taxing (except as an instance of general scepticism about predicting the unexamined on the basis of the examined). We only have to start opening heads.

That something has gone wrong here ought to be apparent because the issue of *solipsism* seems to have disappeared: there is no question about whether I can make sense of the existence of other brains, even if there is a sceptical question about whether there are any. Let us work through this slowly.

As we already know, Sartre is hostile to the idea that the mind is a thing, and also to the idea that conscious episodes are causes of behaviour (see Chapter 2). Instead, he stresses the externalist idea that having-a-mind is a form of embeddedness in an environment. Directedness at intentional objects is a form of activity in a situation involving them. And we have seen reasons for going along with this. But does this not deliver behaviourism by another name? Isn't activity just behaviour? No, because by 'activity' Sartre here means a form of consciousness, and so it is not what behaviourists mean by 'behaviour' (i.e. the capacity for mere bodily movement). 'There is nothing behind the body, but the body is wholly "psychic"' (B&N: 305):

Does this mean that we must grant that the Behaviourists are right? Certainly not. For although Behaviourists interpret man in terms of his situation, they have lost sight of his characteristic principle, which is transcendence-transcended ... Fear is a flight, it is a fainting. These phenomena are themselves not released to us as a pure series of movements but as transcendence-transcended ... This soldier who is fleeing formerly had the Other-as-enemy at the point of his gun ... But behold now he throws his gun in the ditch and is trying to save himself: ... that land in the background, which he was defending and against which he was leaning as against a wall, suddenly opens fan-wise and becomes the foreground, the welcoming horizon towards which he is fleeing for refuge. All this I establish objectively, ... for it is given to us as a new type of internal haemorrhage in the world – the passage from the world to a type of magical existence.

(B&N: 295)

This picks up the idea, last encountered in the previous chapter, and part and parcel of externalism and existentialism, that to understand another as minded involves projecting oneself into their point of view, and seeing the world as they see it. On this approach, to see bodily movement as activity is to see it in a certain way, as the expression of a subject's conscious stance on the world. Seeing someone as minded, that is, involves seeing them *as a subject*, a centre of consciousness, a point of view on the surrounding 'situation', rather than as an object in it.[7] And this brings us back to the reef of solipsism. I can know what it is for you to have a brain, even a brain which is causally embedded in an environment, which makes your mouth emit noises and your eyes swivel in response to environmental changes. *But this is not knowing you as a subject*: and 'the Other must be given to me directly as a subject' (B&N: 253). Recall here the problems of the Picture Gallery Model of Visual Experience (Chapter 6). Conceiving of your brain and its states *as such* gives no clue as to the phenomenology of your experience. So the natural move is to suppose that there are little pictures in the brain (or head), which pictures themselves have phenomenologically present properties. But since this is untenable, homing in on the contents of your skull is no way at all to get at your subjecthood, no way at all to characterise what your experiences and mental life are like.

We may seem to be getting nowhere. We shelved the solipsism issue in order to make progress on the sceptical question, but the most promising answer – that the mind is a causal mechanism responsible for behaviour – has brought us right back to the solipsism. How *can* I know you as a subject? This is where Sartre would make his move. Solipsism keeps appearing on the scene not because the facts require it, but because we are working with inadequate models of the mind. There is not really any problem, he says, about how we understand each other as subjects:

> Descartes has not *proved* his existence. Actually I have always known that I existed, I have never ceased to practise the cogito. Similarly, my resistance to solipsism – which is as lively as any I should offer to doubt the cogito – proves that I have always known that the Other existed, that I have always had a total though implicit *understanding* of his existence, that this 'pre-ontological' *understanding* comprises a surer and deeper grasp of the nature of the Other and the relation of his being to my being than all the theories which have been built around it.
>
> (B&N: 251)

The real issue, he goes on, is that of making clear what this 'understanding' of the Other-as-subject is:

> If the Other's existence is not a vain conjecture, a pure fiction, this is because there is a sort of cogito concerning it. It is this cogito which we must bring to light by specifying its structures and determining its scope and laws.
>
> (ibid.)

Just as I have a direct acquaintance with my own existence as a conscious subject so I have (or can have) a direct acquaintance with the Other's subjective existence. The Problem of the Other is the task of analysing what it is to understand the Other as a subject:

> In my own inmost depths I must find not *reasons for believing* that the Other exists but the Other himself as not being me.
>
> (ibid.)

And given the evident hopelessness of understanding the Other's subjecthood in objective terms, this is surely exactly the right line to take.

Sartre's account of shame just is his analysis of our understanding of subjects, and hence his way of avoiding solipsism. Feeling shame is not like, say, being angry with oneself, since it inelimin-ably involves a mode of my being which is for-another:

> ... the Other has ... established in me a new type of being ...
> [which] was not in me potentially before the appearance of the
> Other, for it could not have found any place in the For-itself.
>
> (B&N: 222)

Shame, unlike anger, presupposes at least the belief that one is (or
could be) *viewed in a certain way* by another person (compare
dishonour, guilt, pride). In other words, this type of self-consciousness presupposes an idea of the other person as a subject with a
view of one, so being self-conscious in this way involves knowing
what it is for there to be another subject. (Hereafter, to retain
harmoniousness with Sartre's locutions, 'the Other' will mean
'another subject' and 'encountering the Other' will mean 'successfully understanding another subject *as* a subject'.)

We need to be cautious about how Sartre's discussion bears on
the sceptical problem of other minds. One might suppose that he
is arguing as follows:

1 Shame requires encountering the Other;
2 I have felt shame on occasions, so;
3 I have encountered the Other (i.e. successfully understood other
  subjects *as* subjects), so I know that other minds exist (or
  have existed).

However, he is not saying this – which is just as well, since this
argument is pretty hopeless. First, it is not clear that feeling shame
requires more than the *belief* that one is encountering the Other. If
so, then although feeling shame would be a way of having an idea
of the Other (of what it is for there to be another subject), and so
would be a demonstration that solipsism is not obligatory, it
would not solve the sceptical problem, since the belief might
always be *false*. Second, it seems open to reply that there could be
another state of mind – call it *schmame* – which is subjectively very
similar to shame but which in fact does not involve the idea of the
Other, but only seems to. Then if I have all along mistaken
schmame for shame, I have never, in fact, even had an idea of what
it is for there to be another subject.

Sartre could reply to the second point that phenomenological
reflection will turn up that it is indeed shame I feel, with its
implicated idea of the Other, rather than schmame. But this leaves
the first point, and is anyway by the by, since he does not really
seem to take the sceptical problem especially seriously. He often

talks as if he has certain knowledge that the Other exists ('the Other is given to me as a concrete evident presence' (B&N: 271) but at other times seems only to make the weaker claim that at least he has the idea of the Other and is *certain* of the Other's existence (one can be certain of what is false). He certainly acknowledges, as he should, that we can be mistaken in thinking we are encountering the Other:

> perhaps the objects of the world which I took for eyes were not eyes; perhaps it was only the wind that shook the bushes behind me.
>
> (B&N: 276)

But if he can be wrong sometimes, why not always? Does this not mean that 'our certainty of the Other's existence take[s] on a purely hypothetical character?' (B&N: 275). He replies that in making such a mistake one is still certain of the Other, and suggests that this is due to our always being 'present' to one another, even when we are physically separated. He links this to the experienced absences we discussed in Chapter 3:

> if I do not find my package of tobacco in its usual spot, I do not say it is absent . . . absence is defined as a mode of being of human-reality.
>
> (B&N: 278)

His thought seems to be that in being aware of one's friend's absence, one is thereby affirming a mutual 'presence', or understanding of each other as subjects.

This is not very persuasive. Given his own claim that an absence 'always appears within the limits of a human expectation' (B&N: 7), it is obvious that one can perceive the absence of the non-human: imagine returning and finding that your bike is not where you left it. In any case, even if his claim about absence were right, an affirmation of my certainty that my friend exists somewhere as a subject is not the same thing as a demonstration of knowledge. Perhaps Sartre's thought is that one can only make mistakes about encountering the Other if one has previously actually had such an encounter. But then the point about absences is irrelevant anyway, and it is not clear why we should accept this latest proposal.[8] On the whole, it seems that Sartre is not arguing from the existence of shame to the existence of the Other. Rather, he is simply *assuming* that we do on occasion encounter Others, and is offering shame as a way in which we do this. His strategy here is parallel to his strategy with anguish and freedom (and nausea and the being of material things). He does not argue from the fact that we feel anguish to the fact that we are free. Rather, he assumes that we are free, and offers anguish as the consciousness we have of this fact.

This point is not affected by the fact that he stresses the *directness* of our intuition of the Other. To call a mode of cognitive access direct is not to say it is infallible: direct realism in perception does not entail that misperception is impossible (otherwise direct realism would be born refuted).

Sartre's attitude to the sceptical problem seems justifiable in the circumstances. Sceptical arguments can be considered just for the sake of it, but they get their urgency from models of the domain in question which seem to make them inevitable. On the Cartesian view of the mind, scepticism about both the 'external' world and other minds seem to fall out immediately. But Sartre is developing a non-Cartesian framework, and so it is far from clear that sceptical worries are inevitable or urgent. Given this, questions such as 'how can we understand others as subjects?' can be taken as requests for epistemological analysis ('how *do* we understand others as subjects?') rather than as the familiar unnerving challenges ('how *could* we understand others as subjects?). Of course, there remains the possibility of arguing that our normal standards for claiming knowledge, as would be evinced by the proposed epistemological analysis, are incoherent or not high enough, and then the sceptical issues would return. But that is a different matter, and no philosopher should be expected to deal with *everything*. Given the traditional Cartesian source of scepticisms, and Sartre's avowed anti-Cartesianism, his procedure seems to me to be above reproach.

## AGAINST SOLIPSISM: THE LOOK

In one sense we see the Other as an object among others. But we see the Other as a special kind of object. This involves recentring: instead of just seeing this man as standing in ordinary spatial relations with other objects, I recognise that these objects are for-him:

there unfolds a spatiality which is not *my* spatiality; for instead of a grouping *towards me* of the objects, there is now an orientation which *flees from me* . . . Thus the appearance among the objects of *my* universe of an element of disintegration in that universe is what I mean by the appearance of a man in my universe.

(B&N: 254–5)

I recognise that, just as these surrounding objects seem to me to group themselves around me, so those selfsame objects seem to him to group themselves around him. This is connected to the fact that, as a subject, he has his own point of view and, in particular, can *look at* these objects, just as I can. Things are objects for-him when he looks at or otherwise apprehends them. But then just as he is an object there to be looked at by me, so I am an object here to be looked at by him. Like anything else, then, I become for-him when he looks at me. But this becoming-an-object-for-him, when I am aware of it, constitutes my understanding of him as a subject. *For things can only be seen as objects by subjects.* Thus, to the extent that I am aware of being an object for-him, I am aware of him as subject:

> It is in and through the revelation of my being-as-object for the Other that I must be able to grasp the presence of his being-as-subject.

(B&N: 256)

Sartre illustrates this view with a typically graphic example. Imagine peeping through a keyhole, totally absorbed in the scenes on the other side. You have no self-awareness (other than the ever-present non-thetic variety), 'there is nothing there but a pure nothingness encircling a certain objective ensemble' (B&N: 260). But then

> all of a sudden I hear footsteps in the hall. Someone is looking at me! What does this mean? It means that I am suddenly affected in my being and that essential modifications appear in my structure.

(ibid.)

> By the mere appearance of the Other, I am put in the position of passing judgement on myself as an object . . . I recognize that I *am* as the Other sees me.

(B&N: 222)

In pricking with the shame of being discovered I understand my discoverer as a subject. *I am* this wretched little creature she can see before her.

This account of Being For-others adds two new types of consciousness to those already discussed. Being For-itself, recall, is essentially thetically aware of intentional objects, and also, in so far as it is conscious, non-thetically self-aware. In feeling shame, now, I acquire a new kind of self-awareness, of myself-as-object, which is routed through the Other's consciousness of me, and which thereby constitutes my awareness of the Other as a subject. Yet these two new modes of awareness are not, properly speaking, knowledge, since knowledge always involves a subject directed on a distinct object, whereas here we have a subject aware of another subject, and also aware of itself as object:

> It is shame or pride which reveals to me the Other's look and myself at the end of that look. It is the shame or pride which makes me *live*, not *know*, the situation of being looked at.
>
> (B&N: 261)

> I experience the unapprehensible subjectivity of the Other directly and with my being.
>
> (B&N: 270)

> The Other-as-subject can in no way be known or even conceived as such.
>
> (B&N: 293)

> [my] body is *lived* and not *known*.
>
> (B&N: 324)

This underlines the point we have come across repeatedly, that in Sartre's view the understanding of conscious phenomena, in this case the Other as such, is a different kind of thing from 'objective' knowledge of things in the environment. It also involves once more 'being's two faces', the tension between our facticity and our transcendence, already encountered in the discussion of bad faith. Somehow I am both subject and object, both radically free and thing-like. The world is both replete with my possibilities and hostile and unyielding. In this particular case, this is due to the Other's freedom:

> each of my free conducts engages me in a new environment where the very stuff of my being is the unpredictable freedom of another.
>
> (B&N: 262)

I experience a 'subtle alienation of all my possibilities' (B&N: 265),

I 'accept the responsibility for this stranger [i.e. me as she sees me]
who is presented to me, but he does not cease to be a stranger'
(B&N: 274). I become 'enslaved' to the Other's view of me (B&N:
267), which is guided by her unknowable freedom, not mine. This
is an aspect of *me* which is beyond my control. At the same time,
although I am revealed to the Other through the appearance to her
of my body, I am not aware of this body as I am aware of other
bodies: I 'live' it. This is all of a piece with the activity-based
conception of conscious mental life: in engaging with intentional
objects I *am* an instrument, the body is not an instrument which I
use, like a hammer (B&N: 323–4).

Sartre's account of Being For-others adds the final crucial
burnish to his activity-based model of consciousness. Rather than
existing as the detached contemplaters of the Cartesian tradition,
for whom even their own bodies are 'external', conscious subjects
exist in an embodied form, one (very special) object among others.
And it is essential to having this type of consciousness that one be
capable of having the idea of the Other, since it is only in virtue of
this that one has a proper grip on the nature of one's own bodily
way of being. In order that I should have a full sense of myself as
a conscious agent, I must be capable of recentring and seeing
myself 'from over there'. But to do this is to be able to envisage a
point of view or subjectivity other than my own as it is here now,
and is hence to escape solipsism (even if not the sceptical problem
of other minds). The thought is not that I usually exist as a *de facto*
solipsist, entirely absorbed in myself and my projects, and only
occasionally step back under pressure from the look and see
things otherwise. Rather, my conception of myself is perpetually
governed by the sense that I am

> outside, in the world . . . a being of the world, like the ego
> of another.
>
> (TE: 31)

Here is yet another aspect of Sartre's denial of the traditional self
or ego. Just as my encounter with the Other is based upon seeing
him or her as a (special) object in my surroundings, so the view
of myself which this encounter makes possible is of a similar
(special) object in these surroundings. The contemplative self of
the Cartesian tradition is completely absent from this picture.

Sartre (sensibly) does not deny that there could be a humanoid
creature lacking this dimension of consciousness, but he claims

that 'this For-itself simply would not be "man"', that is, a person as we understand it (B&N: 282). Such a way of being would not be *our* way of being.

All of this is very hard to quarrel with. Indeed, it seems clear that there are many other ways we have of encountering the Other, and thereby understanding the true nature of our own being, such as in conversation, or as a partner in a shared practical project, and countless other things. But rather surprisingly, Sartre is actually intensely pessimistic about grounding our understanding of subjects in such matters. To this extent, he proceeds to draw conclusions about interpersonal relations from the above which are the opposite of 'hard to quarrel with'. We shall see little reason for going along with him here, and there is evidence that even while working out his pessimistic views he was tempted by the more positive approach to human relationships that he came to hold in his later work.[9] But however this may be, the existentialist conception of conscious mental life we now have before us is plainly much closer to the truth than anything to be found in the Cartesian tradition, including its contemporary manifestation, the computational theory of mind. The question is not *whether* the existentialist conception is on the right lines, but simply how the fine details are to be worked out.

## SORCERERS

We have already come across a notable feature of Sartre's conception of interpersonal relations in the example of the face at the window (Chapter 2). Here, recall, I am suddenly startled or frozen with terror when the face appears, because, says Sartre, 'man is always a sorcerer to man and the social world is primarily magical' (STE: 84–5). He never fully explains his many scattered mentions of magic in this connection, but there appear to be several ideas at work. One is that understanding another (or oneself) as subject is a non-causal kind of understanding. At least as far as the phenomenology of *self*-understanding goes, we are outside the causal order and hence 'magical' (see Chapter 3). But when I encounter the Other, I am, similarly, regarding him or her as a free agent, analogously outside the causal order (this phenomenological claim is compatible with our really being part of the causal order, recall). Minimally, this is a manifestation of the fact that conscious life is end-directed, so that actions need to be understood not in terms of prior causal conditions but in terms of future possibilities:[10]

> From the start I understand his walking in terms of a spatial–temporal ensemble (alley-street-sidewalk-shops-cars, etc.) in which certain structures represent the meaning-to-come of the walking. I perceive this walking by going from the future to the present.
>
> (B&N: 347; cf. 259)

More substantially, we have seen that understanding others as subjects involves a way of seeing them which escapes those who adopt an 'objective' or scientific approach (the present chapter, and the previous one). Relatedly, the relation between subjects and their intentional objects is also allegedly mysterious or extra-causal:

> The relations which I establish between the Other's body and the external object are *really* existing relations, but they have for their being the being of the For-others; they suppose a centre of intra-mundane flow in which knowledge is a *magic* property of space, 'action at a distance.' From the start they are placed in the perspective of the Other-as-object.
>
> (B&N: 305; cf. 167ff., 272)

This is particularly so in cases like emotion, where we project our disgust or fear on to the intentional object and perceive it as objectively disgusting or fearful. Thus Sartre contrasts the claim 'I find him hateful *because* I am angry' with the more usual, and phenomenologically more accurate, 'I am angry because *he* is hateful' (STE: 91).

In so far as we are in this way phenomenologically free and extra-causal, we are also to a degree mysterious and unpredictable to each other. The face at the window is terrifying precisely because

> it is presented, motionless though it is, as acting at a distance. The face outside the window is in immediate relationship with our body; we are living and undergoing its signification . . . The behaviour which gives its meaning to the emotion is no longer *our* behaviour.
>
> (STE: 86–7)

As in the case of being observed spying through the keyhole, we are suddenly aware of ourselves as vulnerable objects in the world of another subject. Our surroundings, formerly suffused with our own possibilities and seen in familiar deterministic means/end terms, 'flee' from us:

> the ensemble 'instrument-possibility', made up of me confronting the instrument, appears to me as surpassed and organized into a world by the Other. With the Other's look the situation escapes me, ... *I am no longer master of the situation* ... [which has an] unpredictable but still real *reverse side*.
>
> (B&N: 265)

## THE WHOLE USELESS PASSION

This element of threat from the Other pervades personal relationships, according to Sartre. The instability of the For-itself's existence as both subject and object, transcendence and facticity, spills over into an instability in how we relate to one another (cf. B&N: 408). On the one hand, 'I can turn back upon the Other so as to make an object out of him', and in this way reject, for example, the shameful object I am for him. Or I can try to assimilate him as a subject, thereby appropriating to myself 'that freedom which is the foundation of my being in-itself [as shameful]' (B&N: 363). The relationship is a perpetual battle between us to assert a sort of mastery in one of these two ways: 'Conflict is the original meaning of being for-others' (B&N: 364). Sartre's example of the second kind of assimilation is love. In loving I exercise my freedom, yet at the same time I want to be loved. But to be loved is not simply to be the object of a sort of mechanical wanting. Rather, it is to be similarly valued as the result of an exercise of freedom:

> Thus the lover does not desire to possess the beloved as one possesses a thing; he demands a special type of appropriation. He wants to possess a freedom as a freedom.
>
> (B&N: 367)

But this is impossible: the more the Other appears to me as subject, the more I am mere object-for-them, and vice versa – 'hence the lover's perpetual insecurity' (B&N: 377). To the extent that I am a mere object for another, I descend into masochism, the 'abyss of the Other's subjectivity' (B&N: 378). But this too is unstable, since my real objective is to be 'fascinated by my self-as-object' (ibid.). That is, the very attempt to abase oneself before the Other presupposes a transcending project of one's own:

> Even the masochist who pays a woman to whip him is treating
> her as an instrument.
>
> (B&N: 379)

Sartre considers several examples of the first kind of assimilation
mentioned above, trying to regard the Other purely as object. One
is indifference or other-blindness, where I 'practise a sort of factual
solipsism' (B&N: 380), and act as though I were the only person in
the world. Others appear to me and are treated as complex
mechanisms in my surroundings, to be avoided or manipulated as
need be, no different in kind from thunderstorms and slot-
machines. Most people regard others like this for at least some of
the time, and here we get one of the sources of bad faith discussed
in Chapter 4: '"people" are functions: . . . the café waiter is nothing
but the function of serving the patrons' (B&N: 381). The waiter
himself might try to enact this view of him, thereby falling into
bad faith. At the same time, I cannot escape 'an implicit understanding' of his freedom, so I am also in bad faith, and my
indifference or blindness is tinged with anxiety. This may lead to
impossible projects of attempting to 'get hold of the Other's free
subjectivity through his objectivity-for-me' (B&N: 382). Sartre
considers sexual desire to be such a project. Characteristically,
he stresses the intentionality of this: desire in its original and
unreflective form is desire for a transcendent object, just like any
other state of mind. It is true that one can reflect upon the nature of
this desire and upon the kinds of outcome which satisfy it, and so
come to desire orgasm, the thrill of 'conquest', or some other
associated pleasure. But this is only possible because there is an
original desire directed at an intentional object (cf. B&N: 557).
Which object? The simple answer is: the Other's body. But this is
too simple, for complementary reasons. First, it is not exactly I-as-
consciousness who does the desiring, since sexual desire, unlike,
say, thirst or hunger, 'takes me over'. Lusting after another person
is not much like being really hungry, though perhaps a bit more
intense. Here more than anywhere else I am aware of my bodily
nature: more, 'the being which desires is consciousness making
itself body' (B&N: 389).[11] Second, by the same token, what I desire
is the Other not as agent but 'incarnated' or made flesh:

> I make her enjoy my flesh through her flesh in order to compel
> her to feel herself flesh. And so possession truly appears as a
> double reciprocal incarnation. Thus in desire there is an attempt

at the incarnation of consciousness . . . in order to realise the incarnation of the Other.

(B&N: 391)

But sadly, 'desire is itself doomed to failure' (B&N: 396). We cannot really dissolve like this into flesh, and even as I try to do it my transcendence reasserts itself and my partner 'falls from the level of flesh to the level of pure object' (B&N: 398). Hereabouts is sadism, the attempt to 'incarnate the Other through violence' rather than by way of my own incarnation (B&N: 399). But this cannot work either, because my victim always remains able to fix me with a look and hence surpass me. Thus 'sadism and masochism are the two reefs on which desire may founder' (B&N: 404): either I try to abase myself as object for the Other, or I try to debase the Other. Either way I fail. A third and yet more desperate option is hate, whose project is 'the realization of a world in which the Other does not exist' (B&N: 410). But this cannot really succeed either, since even as I rid myself of the Other, so I must acknowledge that there have been Others, for whom I have been – and so in a sense am – an object. As Sartre sees it, all other forms of interpersonal relationship are 'enrichments of these [three] original attitudes . . . they all include as their skeleton . . . sexual relations' (B&N: 404).

What a sorry business this all is! But surely, even though there is undoubtedly something that rings true in Sartre's account, we at least sometimes manage better than this. Most people would not agree that sexual relationships have to be as fraught and unsatisfying as Sartre insists, and whether or not sexual relations are, as it were, at the bottom of all others, still many of us seem often to rub along rather more harmoniously than Sartre would have it, in and out of bed. He does consider various types of fellow-feeling which seem to belie his claims (B&N: 413–30) but brushes them aside as parasitic on his own 'original attitudes'. It is hard not to see here plain autobiography, and/or Sartre the novelist, intent on embodying a powerful though partial view of the human condition.

Of course, it may be that these pessimistic conclusions do not really follow from his account of Being For-others: and as remarked above, there seem to be plenty of other ways of encountering the Other besides the essentially antagonistic ones he focuses on. But if these conclusions did follow from his account, then that would be so much the worse for it. So it is worth recalling that an essential component of it does not hold up anyway. Phenomenologically speaking, we do not feel as free as Sartre claims we do: options which should be live too often strike us as dead, or merely theoretical. If so, then the Other need not be so unpredictable and threatening as all that. It is often painful and unnerving to have to cope with the version of oneself that the Other works with, and one is constantly tempted to blot it out in typical acts of self-deception (recall Sartre's homosexual of Chapter 4). But to the extent that the Other is not continually remaking and reassessing in the fashion urged by Sartre, the version of oneself can be expected to remain relatively fixed, and one may thus sometimes learn to live with it. Consequently, there is scope for co-operation and mutual reinforcement as well as for the ontological conflicts dramatised by Sartre. True, if you happen upon me looking through the keyhole, then you may alienate my possibilities: the dark corner where I might have cringed is illuminated by your consciousness of it. It is not so obvious that you would in another type of situation necessarily be threatened by my pride for example, or that I would deflate under your gaze, and anyway Sartre assumes that you wouldn't as soon take a peek yourself. For if your tastes also run to voyeurism, you might actually enhance my possibilities by promising to lend me your binoculars in exchange for a turn at the keyhole. Not the revolutionary sixties, but the caring sharing nineties.

## NOTES AND FURTHER READING

1   J.-P. Sartre, *The Reprieve* tr. E. Sutton (Harmondsworth: Penguin, 1962): 168.
2   See A.J. Ayer, *The Problem of Knowledge* (Harmondsworth: Penguin, 1956).
3   For an elegant discussion of solipsism see D. Pears, *The False Prison* vol. 1 (Oxford: Oxford University Press, 1987): 34–43.
4   If this criticism is just, Descartes is less entitled than he normally thinks to his claim to have an idea of God: and this threatens his entire anti-sceptical argument. Uncertainty on this point does indeed surface at times, as when he concedes that our idea of God is not fully adequate: see the reply to Hobbes' Objection Eleven in, for example, *Descartes: Philosophical Writings* tr. G.E.M. Anscombe and P.T. Geach (London: Nelson, 1954): 143.
5   See H. Putnam, 'Other minds', ch. 17 of his *Mind, Language and Reality* (Cambridge: Cambridge University Press, 1975).

6 For a lucid treatment of such matters, see J. Fodor, *Psychological Explanation* (New York: Random House, 1968).

7 Compare T. Nagel, *Mortal Questions* (Cambridge: Cambridge University Press, 1979) ch. 14, and G. McCulloch, 'Scientism, mind and meaning', pt. II, in *Subject, Thought, and Context* ed. P. Pettit and J. McDowell (Oxford: Oxford University Press, 1986).

8 A favourite anti-sceptical argument used to be that one cannot judge something wrongly to be a so and so unless one can on occasion judge something correctly to be a so and so. Often this took the form of the claim that, for example, there could not be fake banknotes unless there were real ones. But this is not so: due to a massive fraud, there might never have been any real notes officially minted, so that all notes in circulation are in fact fake. All this story needs is the *idea*, or *definition*, of a real note.

9 See J. Simont, 'Sartrean ethics' and T. Flynn, 'Sartre and the poetics of history', both in *The Cambridge Companion to Sartre* ed. C. Howells (Cambridge: Cambridge University Press, 1992).

10 Sartre may well have thought that the end-directedness of psychological explanation precludes it from being causal explanation not only in the phenomenological sense (we standardly explain behaviour by mentioning future (or merely possible) occurrents rather than prior causes), but in every sense (thus see STE: 54). And this was something of an orthodoxy in the mid-century period (thus see the references discussed by D. Davidson, 'Actions, reasons and causes', essay 1 of his *Essays on Actions and Events* (Oxford: Oxford University Press, 1980). Contemporary orthodoxy tends to agree with Davidson that the phenomenological claim is compatible with the factors cited in psychological explanation actually being causal: see G. Macdonald and P. Pettit, *Semantics and Social Science* (London: Routledge, 1981) ch. 2. But for thought-provoking dissent from this, see M. Morris, *The Good and the True* (Oxford: Clarendon Press, 1992) chs. 8 and 12. And the riposte that, even if *the light's being on* is a future occurrence when I *act*, still my *intending to switch the light on* really is a prior causal antecedent of the act, is too simple. It misses the fact that in seeing me as *wanting to switch on the light* one leaves the plane of providing ordinary causal explanation, and starts to engage in understanding me as a subject.

11 For an unusually sensitive account of these matters see R. Scruton, *Sexual Desire* (London: Weidenfeld & Nicolson, 1986).

# Index